CH

CHEATING

What Experts are Saying about

CHATTING or CHEATING

Dr. Sheri Meyers has written a profound and powerful book that is a must-read for anyone wanting to protect your relationship, heal it if it's on shaky ground, or recover from the heartbreak of infidelity. With deep insight, clarity and compassion, she offers you an essential map through the murky maze of the most painful issues a couple can face. *"Chatting or Cheating"* will be the answer to many prayers.

BARBARA DE ANGELIS, PH.D.
#1 NY TIMES BESTSELLING AUTHOR OF *HOW DID I GET HERE?*

"Chatting or Cheating" is a lifeline, giving hope and effective strategies that can help couples recover and rebuild a healthier, happier, more deeply intimate relationship after an affair. I highly recommend reading this book.

DANIEL G. AMEN, M.D., AUTHOR OF *NY TIMES* BESTSELLER
CHANGE YOUR BRAIN, CHANGE YOUR LIFE

Read this book BEFORE you have an affair. Read this book if you've ever fantasized about having an affair. And if you've had an affair, or suspect your partner, read this book to prepare yourself for a journey into intimacy. Thanks to the expertise of Dr. Meyers and her straight-arrow and heartfelt advice, this gem may just save your relationship before trouble even ensues.

MARK ROBERT WALDMAN, AUTHOR OF
HOW GOD CHANGES YOUR BRAIN.

"Chatting or Cheating" is an informative, practical guide for dealing with infidelity. There are wonderful sections on instructing the cheater how to confess and to end an affair—also on how "the betrayed" can recover. This book is filled with useful, straightforward instructions to heal a wounded heart."

JUDITH ORLOFF., M.D., AUTHOR OF
EMOTIONAL FREEDOM

"Chatting or Cheating" offers a complete map from breakdown to breakthrough covering every imaginable circumstance from A to Z, including detecting an affair, dealing with an affair, healing from the betrayal of an affair, to rising from the ashes—like the phoenix bird—by strengthening your relationship with skills and muscles essential for secure partnerships. The layout of the book makes it supremely user friendly; and is a surprisingly easy read for such a difficult topic. Dr. Meyers book is a valuable resource that I highly endorse to anyone who is confused, distressed, in pain, and seeking answers.

GRETA HASSEL,
LICENSED MARRIAGE & FAMILY THERAPIST

Dr. Sheri Meyers book, *"Chatting or Cheating"* is a highly contemporary look at relationship dynamics that have deep implications to marriages and committed relationships. This thought-provoking book vividly illustrates some of the slippery pitfalls that lead a person from seeming innocent flirting (over coffee or over cyberspace) to actions that damage families, loved ones, self-esteem, and the course of one's life.

Written in a non-technical and very readable form, *"Chatting or Cheating"* is an essential for all therapists, and a must read for anyone who wonders about the health of their committed relationship. I'm very impressed with the tremendous contribution this book will make to our profession and to couples everywhere.

PETER LAMBROU, PH.D., AUTHOR OF
CODE TO JOY: THE FOUR-STEP SOLUTION TO UNLOCKING YOUR
NATURAL STATE OF HAPPINESS

"*Chatting or Cheating*" is a must read for anyone whose relationship has been impacted by infidelity. It is an invaluable hands-on guide through the landmine of discovering and responding to your partner's affair. As a divorce lawyer and mediator, I regularly deal with the trauma and loss of broken marriages that result because one partner started out chatting and ended up cheating. If there's a chance you are in those circumstances, "*Chatting or Cheating*" is the light that can lead you and your mate out of the darkness and into the possibility of reconciliation and healing. I highly recommend it.

DENNIS A. COHEN, ESQ.
FAMILY LAW ATTORNEY & MEDIATOR

"Finally, someone has written an easy-to-utilize book that has the most-accurate 21st century clues and insights on why people begin to stray and what can be done to strengthen your love and closeness. If you've ever started to wonder if your relationship is in even the slightest danger, this book can help you sort out truth from self-deception and teach you the ways to build the kind of trust, intimacy and satisfaction you've always longed for. What I found most helpful in this easy-to-utilize book is that the author truly understands the confusing feelings and important steps for knowing when you've started to cross over into a danger zone and how to repair the relationship in a smart, loving way. This book will save many people from painful break-ups and help many couples strengthen their love and closeness."

LEONARD FELDER, PH.D., AUTHOR OF
MAKE UP OR BREAK UP:
8 CRUCIAL STEPS TO STRENGTHENING YOUR RELATIONSHIP

CHATTING
or
CHEATING

*How to Detect Infidelity, Rebuild Love,
and Affair-Proof Your Relationship*

SHERI MEYERS, PSY.D.

Chatting or Cheating
By Sheri Meyers, Psy. D

Published by From The Heart Media, Inc, Tarzana, CA
www.fromtheheartmedia.com
www.chattingorcheating.com

Neither the publisher nor the author is engaged in rendering professional advice or services to the individual reader. The ideas, procedures, and suggestions contained in this book are not intended as a substitute for consulting with a family counselor, psychological professional or physician. All matters regarding the health and wellness of your family members require professional supervision. Neither the authors nor the publisher shall be liable or responsible for any loss, injury, or damage allegedly arising from any information or suggestion in this book. The opinions expressed in this book represent the personal views of the author and not of the publisher, and are for informational purposes only. This book is not intended to replace appropriate counseling, diagnosis, treatment, or other therapeutic intervention, when necessary, by a qualified mental health, physician or other qualified professional.

The events depicted in this published work are fictitious. Any similarity to any person living or dead is merely coincidental.

Cover design by Kim Leonard of Bookcovers.com, used by permission
Text design, styling and formatting by Guy Blews, used by permission
Author portrait by Starla Fortunato, used by permission

ISBN 13: 978-0-9847348-2-5
Library of Congress Control Number: 2012930810

This book is dedicated to the brave and beautiful couples I have personally counseled over the last 25 years who have successfully weathered the 9.0 earthquake (and aftershocks) that occurred with the discovery of infidelity. Thank you for your trust and for allowing me to guide and walk with you on the journey to recovery and greater love.

ACKNOWLEDGEMENTS AND GRATITUDE

The spaces between your fingers were created so that another's could fill them in.

I am GRATEFUL to all the beautiful souls in my life who inspired me, helped me and held my hand in a myriad of ways as I learned life's lessons - ALL of whom have opened my heart to KNOW LOVE. My heart, life (and book) are better for knowing you. Thank you.

No woman is an island, it takes a village to raise a child... and a book.

First and foremost, I deeply respect and owe a huge debt of gratitude to my editor extraordinaire and talented book alchemist, GUY BLEWS, who took my words that were laying dead on the page and brought them to life. Where others had given up he believed, he saw, he conquered, and he created magic, over and over again. Thank you for patiently hanging in there through all my 'first book neurotic changes', pushing me forward and brilliantly transforming my words into music for the mind and heart. Thank you for holding my hand every step of the way. You are brilliant!

Sending my deep, profound gratitude to KIM LEONARD and her team (CASEY, MICHELLE, RICHARD and KELLY) at Bookcovers. com who patiently, lovingly, and creatively helped design the finished interior of my book and ALLEN D'ANGELO who has been my go-to, answer man at AEI Publishing. Big thanks to LISA DESPAIN at ebookconverting.com, who put together my ePub and fastidiously typeset the final edits and changes to my book.

While this book has been a true labor of love, one never knows it's worth until you get unbiased feedback from your peers. Thank YOU so much for the beautiful reception and welcoming to the world that you gave my 'baby'... BARBARA De ANGELIS, DANIEL AMEN, JUDITH ORLOFF, LEONARD FELDER, PETER LAMBROU, DENNIS COHEN, GRETA HASSEL and MARK ROBERT WALDMAN.

I am grateful for all my heart igniting relationship sparks - my family and dear friends, who sit with me around the campfire of love, singing songs, pushing the limits and filling in the missing pieces to the puzzle that is my heart.

My son and daughter, CHRIS and CLAIRE. It is said that we only learn to love by loving. You've both taught me more about standing resolute in unconditional love than anyone else in my life. Your births brought new meaning to what life and love is all about and helped me to join with what is deepest in myself. You are the most precious beings on this planet.

My dad, HAL MEYERS for saying, "I'll believe it when I see it" and pushing me to be a woman of action, not just words. Thank you for being the family's anchor, rock and leader. You taught me what standing tall in resolute LOVE truly means and what "I've got your back" really entails.

And, JAN MEYERS - your femininity, gracious hospitality, love of writing, and talent for creating beauty has been an inspiration to me throughout my life.

JONATHON ASLAY who lovingly encouraged, pushed and unconditionally supported me through every step of the process of writing this book. Thank you for shining your beautiful heart light, holding down the emotional fort, and continually believing in me. You showed me firsthand what it means to live the words, "I am here. You are important. WE matter."

DAVID YOUNG - our friendship has survived the winds of change and the tests of time. Thank you for your generous, loving heart and for all the creative and expansive ways you continually show your care. You have permanent residency in my heart.

I also want to acknowledge with love my family, extended family, and friends — DENNIS MEYERS, MAX & KATIE MEYERS, NICK & BEA LIEBERMAN, BLUE LIEBERMAN, SIRAH VETTESE, DENNIS C., BARRY LEONARD, ALAN SINGER, ALAN COLE-FORD, MONTY TURNER, LYNN IANNI, and SHAYNA LESTER.

Thanks to my early editors JILL EASTON, and DARA HOLLAND; proof-readers NIKI PAYNE, HOLLY HOWARD, BARBARA GLATT, and LORI LATIMER, go-to experts KARA OH and ROBIN COLUCCI HOFFMAN; and beautiful photographer extraordinaire who took my back cover photo STARLA FORTUNATO.

Big hugs of thanks to JACQUIE JORDAN at TVGuestperts and her great group of media goddesses — JANE SHAYNE & STEPHANIE COBAIN and DARICE FISHER at DFI Public Relations.

Special thanks and great love to LYSA BARRY and ANGELA GIACOBBE - two fabulous PR moguls who got the ball rolling by introducing me to Network Television all those years ago and who continue to support me. Not only are you Heavenly Angels, you have both become dear friends.

In the succulent rhythm of right now, I bow in gratitude and say my wholehearted THANKS.

TABLE OF CONTENTS

Chapter 10: Communication: Essential Skills for Your Relationship Tool Kit 167

Chapter 11: Trust Is A 2-Way Street 203

Chapter 12: Forgiveness Leads To Healing 211

INTRODUCTION

How does chatting become cheating?

Imagine this...

You weren't looking for it but then you innocently meet someone, maybe at work, on a business trip, at the health club, a high school reunion, your child's soccer practice, at a class, online, in a chat room, or on Facebook. Something between you just clicks! You spend hours talking, texting, and chatting about anything and everything. It doesn't matter. All you know is that you feel amazing and so do they!

You've never had so much in common with someone, or at least that's what it feels like. You share yourself openly and honestly with no fear of being judged, advised, or criticized. It feels so absolutely right that you can hardly believe it! It's like you're talking with your best friend on earth and you know they really get you!

You walk around smiling from ear-to-ear. You can't stop thinking about them. You create reasons to connect and say hi.

Suddenly, without realizing it, more and more of your attention, time, excitement, and affection is focused toward your new Friend instead of your primary partner, or even your family. Your highs and lows are based on the amount of contact the two of you are having with each other.

You convince yourself that it's just an innocent friendship and because it feels so good, you ignore the truth of what's really going on. All those emotional connections, the long, intimate talks where you share things you should only be discussing with your significant other, the late night, 'just thinking of you' flirty texts are not signs of just an innocent friendship. **It's an affair.**

It can happen to you; it can happen to your partner; it happens to people who would never cheat. But no matter how you (or your partner) may be rationalizing, justifying, or defending your actions, I'm here to alert you that there is danger lurking in the shadows of this so-called Friendship, a danger, so hidden, so unacknowledged that when it unleashes its full force in your life, it can hit you and your relationship like a 9.0 earthquake -- a shock that very well may shake your world down to the ground.

With the rampant use and ease of technology, meeting, staying connected, getting intimate and cheating have never been easier or more dangerous. Dangerous, because an innocent friendship between two people who intend to chat NOT cheat, text NOT flirt, be Friends on Facebook NOT lovers, can quickly evolve into MORE and engulf a person who never intends to cheat.

From the early awakening of desires or knowledge that may seem too exciting or awful to contemplate, to the painful and horrifying realization that there is something going on outside of your relationship, on to the difficulty of a confession, and finally the search for a solution, I am here to offer you reasons, answers and options that will help you cope with the discovery and recovery when a **cyber, physical** or **emotional** affair shakes the very foundation of your relationship.

Whether you are the cheater or the one betrayed, or just curious and wondering if you or your partner are slipping off the edge of a too-close friendship into a full-fledged affair, I'm here to assist you take off the blinders of affair-denial and teach you how to become affair-aware.

I will help you deal head-on with understanding and coping with all aspects of an affair, whether it is **cyber, physical,** or **emotional**. I'll help you see how it began, flourished and evolved; I'll talk you through the brain chemistry that is the source of so many problems; I'll offer you practical and effective methods to reverse the neglect you or your partner are experiencing in your relationship; and I'll help you fight the enemies of intimacy you will need to defeat.

This book has been written to help you and your relationship succeed, instead of die a painful death. I want you to consider this book as your Relationship Rescue and Rehab Manual. It is designed to take you step-by-step, through the process of awakening, realizing, discovering, confronting, (or confessing), healing from betrayal, rebuilding trust, and eliminating the obstacles to love so you can both overcome the disaster of **INFIDELITY**, and safely fall in love with each other again.

Eagerly, from a place of love and compassion, I offer a variety of my tried-and-true methods that have worked for hundreds of couples in my practice, and can work for you as well.

Overcoming **INFIDELITY** is a process, a process that takes time and dedication; dedication to your partner, dedication to your relationship, and most of all a dedication to love, possibly like you've never loved before.

When you apply the easy-to-follow, straightforward strategies I offer in this book, you will have a more loving, honest, and fulfilling partnership on the other end.

Allow me to hold your hand on this journey, and together we will get you through this.

From my heart to yours,

Part 1

WHEN CHATTING BECOMES CHEATING

When does a friendship become more than a simple friendship? When does an innocent acquaintance turn into something extra? When does a relatively platonic situation evolve into a deeper connection?

How do you know if there is someone else?

How do you know if your partner has crossed the line?

When does CHATTING become CHEATING?

When Emotional Sex takes over.

CHAPTER

1

WHAT IS EMOTIONAL SEX?

EMOTIONAL SEX is a phrase I have coined over my years of practice as a licensed relationship therapist that describes how one or both partners are irresistibly drawn to people who they initially thought of as 'friends.'

EMOTIONAL SEX happens when you feel that someone else gives you what you are missing in your primary relationship, and because of this you channel the bulk of your emotions, hopes and desires onto the other person.

EMOTIONAL SEX is the unspoken attraction, the deeply rooted need to bond, attach, and feel loved that turns a friendship into an affair.

EMOTIONAL SEX is at the heart of what unconsciously draws us to make emotional choices and act in ways that are contrary to our ideals, values, and relationship goals.

EMOTIONAL SEX is an affair of the heart that feels the same as romantic love and can manifest itself in numerous ways - physically, chemically, romantically, emotionally, lustfully, verbally, even cyberly.

EMOTIONAL SEX involves a great deal of deception, lies, and betrayal, sometimes even more than a purely physical affair.

EMOTIONAL SEX involves a person's heart and feelings.

EMOTIONAL SEX is extremely damaging to a relationship.

EMOTIONAL SEX comes in so many disguises, often in the form of a seemingly innocent friendship. It can be so well-hidden, so unacknowledged, so denied, that when it unleashes its full force on your life and your relationship, it feels like you have been hit by a runaway train.

EMOTIONAL SEX is A NEW FORM OF INFIDELITY.

Whether it starts with a seemingly meaningless cyber chat, or an innocent cup of coffee with a workmate, playmate or a best friend's partner, the seductive chemistry of **EMOTIONAL SEX** can take over. And before you know it, it can overrule your better judgment, consume your mind, steal your heart and then steadily destroy your primary relationship.

Most of us think we'd NEVER Cheat
Think again

Since many affairs occur with a genuine friend, it is often difficult to distinguish between an affair and an innocent friendship...

Friends and lovers often behave and communicate in similar ways - they talk, text, have lunch together, give one another gifts and confide in each other. They offer time, attention, acknowledgement and meet each other's emotional needs. That is why it is so easy for friends of the opposite sex to fall in love.

It can happen to **you.**
It can happen to **your partner.**

None of us are strangers to the ever-increasing rates of **INFIDELITY**. If you have not seen the actual statistics, you have most certainly heard about it or have even experienced it for yourself. But now, you have a more seductive arena to be aware of—**EMOTIONAL SEX**.

INFIDELITY has been common since the dawn of time. But in today's world, with the 24/7 constant and consistent use of cyber technology that allows us to immediately connect with anyone at anytime, you are more prone than ever to being the victim of **EMOTIONAL SEX.**

If you are in the early stages of **wondering** whether you are falling for someone, or if your partner is falling for someone else, this book will give you the ability to either control the situation you are getting into or guide your partner away from the path they are taking.

If you are in the midst of an **affair**, this book will give you answers as well as a calm, rational, healing way to: confess the liaison; gracefully exit without drama; end the affair with honesty and clarity; and then deal with the trauma of loss so you can heal with your partner.

If your partner and relationship has taken the plunge into a nightmare you never thought would happen to you, this book will give you hope and the tools required to help you and your partner deal with and overcome the pain of cheating.

**Together, we can overcome the threat of
EMOTIONAL SEX.**

---

*You can actually have deeper,
            more honest love on the other end of this*

WHAT IS CHEATING?

When one partner violates the other's expectations about what is appropriate for the relationship, the second partner feels betrayed.

CHEATING, and how much contact you think is appropriate for your partner to have with a person of the opposite sex—and under what circumstances—can vary widely from person to person in a relationship. You and your partner have come to this relationship with your own beliefs, expectations and definitions about what cheating is and means. Have you ever sat down and clearly told each other the specifics?

I often hear clients and friends describe **CHEATING** in broad strokes, such as, *"CHEATING is when you have sex with another person other than me."* While having sex with another is high on most lists, what about all the other things besides sex? I bet that there are dozens of behaviors your partner could do that would leave you feeling betrayed, shaken, jealous, and upset.

Nowadays, women and men are sending each other flirty texts, becoming friends with their ex on Facebook, getting overly close to each other at work and staying in contact after work hours. When does your partner's behavior (and—hello!—yours) cross the line into the this-is-NOT-cool **CHEATING** territory?

*It's a lot easier to **deceive yourself** and **your partner** about cheating*

*when the **ground rules** of your relationship are **murky***

Let's define YOUR rules, so we can pinpoint what **CHEATING** means to you in your relationship. Here are some ideas to get you started. Check all that apply...

It is unacceptable for my partner to:

➋ Flirt with others (i.e. send signals that they are romantically available or interested).

➋ Discuss confidential things about our relationship with a member of the opposite sex.

➋ Share their most private thoughts and feelings with someone else and not me.

➋ Tell other people he/she is single.

➋ Discuss sexual desires and fantasies with someone other than me.

➋ Regularly exchange 'personal' emails or text messages with an ex.

➋ Be emotionally or sexually intimate with someone other than me.

➋ Socialize with a person of the opposite sex without me.

➋ Purchase intimate gifts for others whom I don't know about.

➋ Engage in and become sexually aroused by online pornography, sexual chat rooms, or IM conversations.

➋ Develop a crush or feelings for someone else, even if not acted on.

➋ Become a best friend or activity partner with someone of the opposite sex that excludes me.

➋ Fantasize about someone else while having sex with me.

➋ Send or receive sexually explicit photos, messages, IM's or texts.

It is important for you and your partner to sit down and find out if you both share the same definition about what constitutes **CHEATING**. Defining **CHEATING** for yourself and your partner helps create boundaries. Crossing those boundaries is what leads us to feeling betrayed - which is what **CHEATING** is really all about.

When you are both clear on what types of actions and behaviors constitute cheating, and you both honor and commit to being faithful to that definition, then the chances of unknowingly sliding down the slippery slope of betrayal into **EMOTIONAL SEX** will be minimized.

WHY WOULD MY PARTNER CHEAT?

As a therapist, I'm often asked, "Why would my partner cheat?"

My answer:

> *"An affair is generally a symptom of an underlying problem in your relationship - either consciously or subconsciously, your partner feels something is missing. And this missing element makes your partner vulnerable to temptation from whomever - the sexy co-worker, the attentive fellow parent who's always up to listen to them vent about work or parenting issues, a new friend on Facebook, the contractor who's going through a divorce and tells tales that resonate for your partner. Affairs, especially cyber affairs, may start innocently enough."*

A partner cheats because there is vulnerability, either personally or in your relationship. Problems can occur if your relationship has become stagnant, if you are not interacting with each other, if sex is a thing of the past, or if there have been changes that have directed a lot of attention and energy away from the relationship.

Your partner may be hungry - for intimacy, for excitement, for companionship, for self-worth and seeks to fill that hunger through other means. Cyber sex, emotional intimacy with coworkers, or a full-blown affair may feed the need.

To get to the heart of the reason for the EMOTIONAL SEX consider CHEATING to be the symptom and not the illness

There are lots of reasons why people cheat. We will get into more details about those reasons later in this section, but here are six of the main reasons why most cheaters say they strayed.

The 6 main relationship problems that lead to INFIDELITY

1. **Feeling Lonely.** If one partner is often away; traveling for work, spending time alone, pursuing separate interests, hanging out with their friends, then the other partner may begin to seek contact and connection elsewhere.

2. **Lack of Communication.** Poor or weak communication causes problems in any relationship. If partners are unwilling or unable to discuss day-to-day problems with one another or take the time to tune in and listen to each other, then the relationship will start to deteriorate rapidly.

3. **Love and Affection Deficit.** One of the most common reasons for adultery is a lack of love and affection.

4. **Boredom, Complacency and Emotional Distance.** Without the exchange of Attention, Affection, and Appreciation the relationship will starve.

5. **A Sexual Disconnection.** If desire is low and there is a lack of sexual connection, then one or both partners may look for excitement outside of the relationship.

6. **Lack of Intimacy.** Without intimacy, no relationship will survive for long.

IS MY PARTNER CHEATING ON ME?

If you're feeling insecure about your relationship, perhaps it's for a good reason. Maybe your partner doesn't seem as available to you, both physically and emotionally. You try to talk and their attention seems to be elsewhere. Maybe they are harder to get a hold of at work, don't respond to your touch in a loving way, or seem detached and preoccupied.

Maybe you've even picked up on some suspicious activity. For example your partner is spending extra time on the computer and texting regularly— but not with you.

➡ How do you know if there's someone else?

➡ When does CHATTING become CHEATING?

➡ And what really constitutes CHEATING anyway?

➡ How do you know if your partner has crossed the line?

If your partner is giving time and energy to someone else, what can you do to confront them about it - and what does it all mean for the future of your relationship?

In fact, where does it start?

The answer: It starts with EMOTIONAL SEX

THE SLIPPERY SLOPE OF EMOTIONAL SEX

The Slippery Slope that leads to cheating is everywhere—INTENSE AND INVISIBLE—waiting, stalking, and watching for the right moment to strike down the faithful intentions of you or your partner.

When does EMOTIONAL SEX begin?

Most of us think that there is a difference between a platonic friendship and a sexual relationship. Most of us think that we **know** the difference. Most of us think we can **control** that difference... **But when does the platonic cross over into the sexual?**

- ❷ Is it when the first words of flirtation are spoken... or written?

- ❷ Is it when there is a physical moment of intimacy?

- ❷ Is it when there is full on intercourse?

If you ask me, it happens in all of the above referenced cases (and then some). No matter how **INFIDELITY** evolves, it always involves secrecy and someone else.

> Did YOU know?
> Affairs 'happen' to non-cheaters ALL THE TIME.
> I've counseled many of them as clients over the years.

One of the pitfalls of **EMOTIONAL SEX** is that it often starts innocently.

For example, you're just chatting—talking lightly with someone at work or with another parent, and because a common environment or interest has thrown you together, you sit down to have a cup of coffee and pass the time.

While **EMOTIONAL SEX** may not lead to actual sex (although it commonly does), **EMOTIONAL SEX** can still be equally intense, sensual and all-consuming. An **EMOTIONAL SEX** situation can wreak the same havoc, mistrust and misgivings on a relationship as full on sexual **INFIDELITY** and may well lead to a break up of the primary relationship.

In actuality, most **INFIDELITY** occurs not because it is planned, but because people find themselves in situations where their emotions completely overwhelm (and even surprise) them.

Surging **brain chemicals** and **hormones** take over

*and once they do, it's a **done deal**... You're* IN

The tendency very often is to dismiss **EMOTIONAL SEX** with "It's just innocent flirting" or "We're only Facebook friends" or "They're simply a co-worker - nothing more!" I hear variations of these excuses from my clients all the time.

BUT THERE IS A BIG DIFFERENCE...

WHEN FRIENDSHIP CROSSES THE LINE FROM **CHATTING** INTO THE **CHEATING** ZONE...

There is a BIG Difference between a *Platonic Friendship* and EMOTIONAL SEX!

Naturally, it's important for everyone to have a strong support system and friendships. However, there is a huge difference between a platonic friendship and a friendship that has crossed the line into the **EMOTIONAL SEX** danger zone. A Platonic Friendship doesn't have the elements of sexual chemistry or attraction. You may love your friend, but you don't fantasize or daydream about him or her. You CAN wait to talk to them. Your relationship with your friend is in the open. Your partner is welcome to join you and your friend, and is not excluded from the friendship because you have nothing to hide.

EMOTIONAL SEX, in contrast, is much more exclusive. There is an element of secretiveness to **EMOTIONAL SEX** that your partner has no part in. You are sharing a significant piece of your emotional life—more about who you are and what you really feel—with your friend than with your primary partner. There is also a strong sexual chemistry or attraction between the two of you, whether you are ready to admit it or not.

A Platonic Friendship is an open friendship that everyone knows about.

> *EMOTIONAL SEX is just the opposite - there is secrecy, there is intimate bonding, there's chemistry, and there is exclusion*

Emotional Sex Scenarios...

"I knew when I crossed the line because I was doing things and sharing myself in ways I'd never tell my boyfriend about, and would freak out if I found out he was doing these exact things with another behind my back." Cheryl

"I knew when I crossed the line because ALL I could think about was him, ONLY HIM. Being with him became more important than my friends, family or husband." Michelle

"I knew I had crossed the line when I found innocent touching, like taking lint off her sweater or accidently touching her hand felt as thrilling as full blown sex with my wife." Frank

"In the midst of caring for three small children and working part-time, e-mailing, texting and talking with Chad felt like an inno-cent escape and a relief. I never would have considered or said that I was in an awful marriage. My husband and I actually got along fine. We just didn't have time to spend alone together as a romantic couple anymore. When Chad and I started chatting on Facebook, I had no intention or desire to cross any physical lines. I would never cheat. But I increasingly found myself shar-ing more and more of my hopes and desires with Chad instead of my husband. I looked forward to my conversations with Chad in a way that was all too consuming. I felt withdrawal when we didn't connect. And it was Chad—not my husband—who was filling me up emotionally and romantically. I now realize that I was unwittingly cheating on my husband—I was having a cyber-emotional affair." Jennifer

Even if you think you know your partner, You don't know EVERYTHING (sometimes that's okay... sometimes not)

HOW FRIENDSHIP TURNS INTO CHEATING

THE BIG WORLD WIDE WEB

With the ever-increasing technology that is available at our fingertips, the world is continually shrinking and expanding:

Expanding in that we can virtually access anyone anywhere in the world from our desks and laptops;

Shrinking in the sense that we can literally access anyone anywhere without ever leaving our house.

The world we desire is but a click away - 24 hours a day, 7 days a week.

It's never been easier or faster to get intimate with someone outside of a committed relationship thanks to websites like Facebook, meet up sites based on common interests like Meetup.com, dating sites like Match.com and infidelity promoting sites like Ashley Madison. And then of course there's chatrooms, texting, sexting, even video-conferencing which allow us to show and tell, not to mention the millions of websites that allow us to access anything our heart, mind or body may desire.

Did YOU know? Facebook is now cited in over 20% of divorces[†]

A spontaneous decision to connect with an old flame, a new "online buddy," or to instant message an acquaintance or coworker, first leads to playful banter, then ever-increasing exchanges, and then suddenly there's that butterfly feeling you get when you fall for someone you barely know (or know too well)......and you can't stop thinking about them. Before you realize it, you find yourself wondering, "how did it ever come to this point?"

What may have begun as a chance encounter or a quick hello has quickly developed into a heart-quickening, full-fledged emotional

[†]Lawyers.com

involvement - a situation with all the trappings, excitement, ups and downs of an affair. And just because it's purely emotional (or cyber) doesn't make it any less illicit or dangerous.

It is shockingly easy to get caught in this kind of situation, to dive head first into all of its digital glory. Feeling aglow (and aghast) with that sudden 'intimate' attention from the opposite sex - attention that feeds a yearning to be attractive, sexy, intelligent, admired, desired. All the things once felt with a partner, but are currently lacking or diminished because, well... because life got in the way and all of a sudden **EMOTIONAL SEX** has begun in the most innocent (and ridiculous) of ways.

Although people trapped in troubled marriages are more vulnerable to **INFIDELITY**, I've discovered that a surprising number of people in seemingly solid relationships have also responded to the novelty of a new love and ended up getting swept away by the emotional tide of something different.

Because it is so beguiling, its boundaries so fuzzy, the EMOTIONAL SEX challenge to a relationship is extremely hard to detect and diffuse - at least initially - but it can most certainly be felt.

Perhaps physical air space has not been shared. Yet.

But this is a dangerous path that could go all the way. The rush generated by a new 'friendship is flammable—a rush that, if fueled by one little indiscretion (i.e. one flirtatious text, one sexy photo sent, one kiss, one too many drinks, one lingering look or transfer of body heat) could ignite an all-consuming passion.

And whether it is you or your partner doing this, your relationship at home is at risk and WILL suffer.

... and there you have it - the slippery slope has been found, the friends card has been played and the **INFIDELITY** has begun...

You may well be asking - Why do people put themselves in a compromising situation to begin with?

If something is NOT right in the primary relationship, why not fix it?

HOW COULD THIS HAPPEN IN MY RELATIONSHIP?

WHY CYBER, PHYSICAL, & EMOTIONAL AFFAIRS HAPPEN

🡒 *We share an address, but little else.* Living in the same house, but in different worlds, does not a relationship make. Let's face it, long-distance relationships are difficult to sustain, and by that I mean relationships characterized by any kind of distance, whether it be physical or emotional. Statistics show that couples who lead separate social lives — separate friends, careers, travel plans, etc. — are much more likely to cheat than couples who spend more of their time together and give each other the 3 A's: Attention, Appreciation, and Affection.

🡒 *Houston, we've got a problem... or two or three.* As problems surface and grow in a relationship, people often avoid facing them and instead take refuge in other people.

Infidelity is more common in relationships where people feel misunderstood or under-appreciated and where fighting, bickering and belittling pass for normal communication. Frequent criticism and complaining about each other (especially to people outside the relationship) shows a lack of respect for your partner and undermines the core foundation and emotional safety in your relationship.

In her 2003 book "NOT Just Friends," psychologist Dr. Shirley Glass found that 82% of unfaithful partners (she counseled) had affairs with someone who was AT FIRST "just a friend"[†]

🡒 *I love my partner, I'm just not "in love" anymore.* This is a fairly common phenomenon. After years of being with the same person and sharing the routines and roles of daily domesticity, couples find that without attention to keeping the spark alive, they have become more like roommates than sex-

[†] Not "Just Friends": Protect Your Relationship from Infidelity and Heal the Trauma of Betrayal (Free Press 2003)

ual partners. When couples stop seeing each other through the eyes of desire; romance and sexual desire declines and emotional separation grows. One or both partners may begin to look for fulfillment and excitement outside of the union to see if they've 'still got it' when it comes to attracting and keeping someone new interested.

➲ *They 'get me' like no other.* If you and your partner aren't sharing mutual values and interests, and you meet someone with whom you do, it makes you feel as if that other person is better suited for you. In fact, they may even seem like the 'soul mate' you never knew existed which, in turn, can fuel doubts about remaining with your partner.

➲ *Not so sweet revenge.* My partner did it to me, and now it's my turn. When one partner cheats, the other may feel they're entitled to do the same. If post-affair healing has never occurred, or is incomplete, the person who was betrayed may seize an opportunity to cheat. When opportunity knocks, they answer—willingly.

People knowingly, and often unknowingly, enter into an affair

➲ *The sweet escape of Internet communication.* It's so easy to emote in the anonymity of your home without the risk of being discovered - plus, the forbidden nature of it all (consciously acknowledged or not) adds to the deliciousness of the communication.

➲ *Ch-ch-ch-changes.* The reasons could be any or many: raising children, midlife crisis, menopause, men-on-pause, seven year itch, financial woes, retirement, illness, loss of job, loss of parents, family pulls and pressures — you name it, it's an excuse turned into a reason.

➲ *The kids may be alright, but what happened to us?* Children may indeed be a blessing, but couples with dual careers often find limited time to spend with each other. Whatever time and energy they have is poured into the kids, to the extent that co-parenting becomes the only glue remaining in the relationship. Child-centered marriages put the real marriage at tremendous risk, as both parties feel isolated from one another and are not having their adult needs met.

➲ *I deserve a little something for ME.* Things are hard, frustrating and/or confusing in your life. You may be working too much, your needs are going unmet, and you feel all you do is sacrifice for others and get nothing in return. An affair is a way to distract yourself from all these difficulties, satisfy some unmet desires and treat yourself to some long overdue pleasure by creating an 'oasis of romance' for yourself.

➲ *I need to feel.* You haven't experienced this much excitement in a long time, if ever. Conversing on the Internet, going out for drinks with a co-worker and relaxing (just the two of you) after a hard day at work is fun. It makes you feel so happy, liked, and good about yourself. Where's the harm in that?

➲ *It's a way of 'checking out' without leaving... yet.* You've given up on your marriage but you're afraid to pull the plug, so you're hoping that an affair will end things for you. It's the 'affair as an exit strategy' with a built-in assumption that either your spouse will discover your infidelity and kick you out, or your lover will give you an ultimatum and/or the courage to leave.

The first step is to recognize that there may be weaknesses in your relationship, as well as a dire need to protect it NOW. Only then can it be brought back to stable footing and given a strong infusion of love and life.

Is your relationship vulnerable to EMOTIONAL SEX & INFIDELITY?

1. Do you long for more emotional and/or sexual attention from your partner at home?

2. Are the two of you spending less time together, either due to children, work, or simply growing apart?

3. When you're with your partner, do you feel bored, detached, or just plain lonely? Do they?

4. Is it hard to talk and connect with your partner about emotions and other things that are important to you? Is it hard for them to connect with you?

5. Do you feel 'bottled up' on the inside - lonely, conflicted, bitter, or angry?

6. Is there a big question mark in your mind and heart about your current relationship?

7. Do you enjoy your friends' partners, and frequently ask yourself, "Why can't my partner be more like so-and-so?"

8. Has there been an increase in fighting in your relationship? Does everything you say to each other seem to push a button?

9. Do you blame your partner for that ever-widening distance between the two of you?

10. Do you feel like the negatives outweigh the positives right now in your relationship, giving you a 'glass half empty' rather than a 'glass half full' attitude?

11. Are you or your partner suddenly wanting to seek stimulation elsewhere, to shake things up, get the excitement pumping, and feel more alive?

12. Are you or your partner hanging around someone who is sexually interested or interesting?

13. Do you or your partner spend hours on the Internet, networking in chat rooms, socializing on Facebook, tweeting, texting, or emailing friends?

The Result:

➡ If you answered **YES** to **1 or 2 questions,** your relationship may not be particularly vulnerable to having an affair - but you can certainly stand to do some work on your relationship. All relationships require nurturing, but by answering YES to 1 or more questions, you've confessed to yourself some dissatisfaction that ought to be addressed. Want a relationship that's vibrant and fulfilling? **WORK AT IT. WORK FOR IT.**

➡ If you answered **YES** to at least **3 questions** - **WARNING** - Your relationship is vulnerable to having **EMOTIONAL SEX.** Awareness is the first step to preventing **INFIDELITY.** This book will help you stop a problem before it develops or learn how to repair the possible damage already done.

➡ If you answered **YES** to more than **5 questions** - RED ALERT You're living in the danger zone. You need to take an honest, fresh look at your relationship and begin the process of repair. If you haven't been engaging often or honestly with your partner, now is the time to swing into action. Don't worry - I will hold your hand. This book has tips and guidelines to get you through the process of detection, confronting, repairing and healing. You can mend your primary relationship with the right tools and motivation.

THE GOOD NEWS IS...

You are now gathering information that will help you save your relationship

---

CHAPTER

2

BECOMING AFFAIR AWARE

The BIG 3 B-AWARES

*Chatting leads to **CHEATING** when emotional doors are opened to deep and desired connections that can be powerful and silent seducers to the vulnerable participant.*

There are 3 B-AWARES that promote EMOTIONAL SEX:

*Emotional Sex has **Breeding Grounds**.*

*Emotional Sex involves **Brain Chemistry**.*

*Emotional Sex thrives on **Boredom**.*

Breeding Grounds: Work, the Internet, and parenting outings are the three biggies where men and women are meeting and spending more time together, both professionally and socially. This creates untold opportunities to become familiar with like-minded people – of both sexes – that come together in an environment that encourages teamwork and sharing. The problem arises when 'teamwork' and common interests bleed over into personal familiarity – **'after hours' socializing, sharing confidences, and personal emailing and texting** can lead to a slippery slope of communication where becoming too familiar leads to boundary breakdowns.

Brain Chemistry: We might think that the brain would be smart about love. That it could be relied upon to intellectualize things and help keep us on the straight and narrow, right? Not so much when we're attracted to someone. Unfortunately, in this case, **the brain is full of chemicals that go berserk when we fall in lust or love,** making affairs the equivalent of a really big chemistry experiment run amok.

Boredom: If we are feeling satisfied and fulfilled within a relationship, even Mr. or Ms. Drop Dead Gorgeous couldn't get our attention — at least not to the point where we would act on any fantasies. But **when life is dull, stressful or just plain predictable**, the seeds of an affair can take root. Fast.

B-Aware #1: Breeding Grounds

EMOTIONAL SEX *has Breeding Grounds—*
The Spaces, Places and Faces that get a relationship into trouble.

In my experience, there are some highly inviting and susceptible breeding grounds where **EMOTIONAL SEX** can sneak up and take a bite—the workplace, cyberspace and playspace, even the sudden re-appearance of an ex.

In a nutshell, if a relationship is vulnerable, temptation can appear anywhere and everywhere. It's on a computer, at work, at reunions, weddings, the grocery store, the gym, sporting events, parties or even at a stop light. Plain and simple, it's hard to escape.

The best defense is to have the knowledge and skills to recognize these breeding grounds and learn to handle any seductive temptation properly whether the victim of an affair is your partner or yourself.

Breeding Ground #1: **Workplace Romances: Don't Give at the Office**

Just because it's work, it doesn't always stop there

The reality is, we spend an inordinate amount of time at work. Both men and women get into the office early and burn the midnight oil, often as colleagues, or in boss/employee or employee/client relationships. In business, the office environment isn't the only place where we spend a large amount of our time. It can also include business trips to meet clients, corporate team-building retreats,

Did YOU know?
62% of married MEN
46% of married WOMEN who strayed, met their lovers through work[†]

[†] http://www.usatoday.com/news/nation/2003-01-08-workplace-usat_x.htm

sales meetings and brainstorming sessions over drinks after work. The boundaries between work and friendship are constantly being challenged.

A new person gets hired and we may be asked to be his or her mentor, show that person the ropes, stay after work to help them assimilate and excel so that the whole team benefits. It's this kind of professional commitment and resulting bonding that prompted author Dr. Shirley Glass to dub the office as **the new minefield for marriage**.

Most of us don't go to work wearing a 'mental metal helmet' and a 'flirting flak jacket'. We aren't on alert, safeguarding against inappropriateness when working with a business colleague. After all, we're just doing business — working together to further the interests of a company or organization.

But business can turn into funny business too easily, especially if we're surrounded by hot, funny and lively people at work.

Emotional Sex Scenario:

"I have had a crush on a co-worker ever since I met him about 3 years ago. It started when he asked me to be friends with his wife because she was depressed and lonely after having moved into the area and she didn't know many people. He would invite my husband and I to their house for movie night. He would sit on the other side of me. I could feel the electricity between us. Then last month, he told me, "I've got a crush on you." I didn't say anything back right then, but we've been texting flirty, sexy messages to each other at work all day long. It certainly makes the day go by. Nothing physical has happened. We talk and have lunch together whenever we can. He tells me that he enjoys our conversations as much as I do. To put the icing on the cake, his wife has now become one of my best friends and often tells me about the problems within their marriage. This is getting very complicated and confusing. I just want to be able to have an innocent friendship with him. I know anything physical is out of the question although I do fantasize about him frequently. My life feels more whole because he's in it."

Breeding Ground #2: **The Sexual and Emotional Embrace of Cyberspace**

Virtual Affairs, CyberChatting, CyberSexing, Sexting

A click to a chat, a chat to a cheat... 24/7

Emotional Sex Scenario:

"I don't want to get divorced, but I like the quick thrill of dating — cyber-dating, actually — during the day. My cyber girlfriend is younger and hotter than my wife, and she makes me feel young and desired. I haven't slept with her and really don't plan to. Heck, we've never even met in person, although I've definitely fantasized about it! Thank God we both have a webcam. There's a lot you can sexually do together and never physically touch. I know I shouldn't be doing this, but it's energizing me during a 15-year marriage that's become boring. In fact, my virtual girlfriend is what makes my marriage bearable."

Once upon a time, the main way to meet someone and start an affair was to get to know them face-to-face. But in today's world where most of us spend hours a day on the Internet, we often 'meet' people virtually. Just look up anyone on Facebook and, unless it's on a private setting, you can learn about his or her interests or location, view personal (often highly revealing) photo albums, and learn volumes about the person's life and lifestyle, including details about their friends and family life, relationship status, and even if they happen to be looking to meet someone special. Often, you don't even have to be an acquaintance (let alone a friend) to get a sense of who they are and what excites them. It's like the ultimate fantasy of being a fly on the wall — in this case, the Facebook wall. Such a voyeuristic thrill... And when it turns out that that person has friends in common, well that creates an opportunity to become instant friends! Doesn't it?

Cyber affairs are so devious because they can be the ultimate fantasy. We may find ourselves in a chatroom where someone is giving us a quickening thrill that comes from attention and intimate conversation—a feeling that may be long gone from our primary relationship.

We can be anyone we want to be. We can reveal the real person that our partner doesn't respond to anymore. *We can project onto this other person's life all the qualities that lack in our own. There is no limit to the imagination.* Sexting, sharing sexy photos and e-cheating is more than just sex—it's about feeling appreciated and good about ourselves.

What's more, the whole interaction is devoid of any real-world distractions, which are so conveniently filtered and left on the side of the screen. In cyberspace, we're staring rapt at the computer monitor or smartphone—not at our spouse asleep in front of the TV, the kids yelling at each other, the pile of dishes in the kitchen sink, or that report left unfinished in another window.

In the cocoon of cyberspace, we can emote easily (and seemingly without consequence), pour out our deepest feelings and connect with someone who shares our interests. When people share and reveal themselves, intimacy develops from the heady mix of mind and emotions. It's not only sexually arousing, it's emotional titillating and captivating.

Did YOU Know?
The vast majority of chatroom interactions are romantic in nature

Suddenly, we can't wait to log on, check our messages and FEEL GOOD throughout the day. It's only Facebook, so there's nothing wrong with it, right? Millions of people are on there, so we're in good company. It's all just about being sociable and friends with someone.

Not necessarily. There's something called **Chat Cheating**. Being online friends with someone and flattering them, commenting on their appearance, their wit, their life. Sharing intimacies. Revealing more and more personal information about yourself. Feeling aroused by the attention and interaction. This is all tantamount to **EMOTIONAL SEX** ... B-AWARE.

flirting is flirting
if it is not okay in real life,
then why is it okay on a computer?

B-AWARE CHECK IN *FOR CHAT CHEATING*

Some people take things even further. They might exchange email addresses or cell phone numbers. Maybe they even arrange to meet online privately in a sex or singles chat room.

 Keeping secrets is not good for you... your partner... or your primary relationship.

How far has it gone?

QUESTIONS to ask your partner if you are suspicious (which are the same questions you should ask yourself if you are being flirtatious):

Have You Ever:

- ❓ Exchanged personal and confidential information (and/or had offline contact) with an online 'friend' that I do not know about?
- ❓ Sent or received a flirtatious email or text?
- ❓ Visited or participated in a sex or singles chat room?
- ❓ Done anything sexual using your webcam?
- ❓ Sexted—i.e. sent a sexy message or photo?
- ❓ Shared your fantasies, masturbated and/or mutually masturbated?

Did YOU Know?
40% of tech savvy adults flirt via e-mail or instant messaging and routinely send sweet and sexy text messages by cell phone [†]

Answering YES to any of the above should set off some blaring alarms in your head that you or your partner are definitely sliding down the slippery slope into the EMOTIONAL SEX **Cheating Zone.**

† *http://www.perfectmatch.com/onlinedating/over50/singles-over-50-dating-tips.asp*

Breeding Ground #3:
Playdates to Playmates
A simple parental chore turns into something more

Emotional Sex Scenario:

"My son was in the lacrosse team and I used to go to the late afternoon practices when my husband couldn't get back from work in time. I noticed one other parent on the bleachers, a father of my son's friend, so I went over to talk to him as he looked a little lonely. Within a few weeks, I realized that I was worrying about the way I looked before I went to the lacrosse practices, and I would look for him whenever I got there. In fact, I began to hope my husband would be delayed at work. Everything was innocent to begin with, the usual chats about kids, school, the area we lived in. But then we started talking well after the practice had finished. Before we knew it we were arranging play dates and quick bites to eat with the kids after the practice. Before long, he and I were looking for ways to spend time alone. And then it crossed the line, and now I am a cheater who cannot seem to stop no matter how much I know it is wrong."

What could be more innocent than parents getting together to cheer on their children's team, take their kids out to dinner after practice, or even get the kids together for some after-school bonding time? There's plenty of time to chat with that nice parent, commiserating or congratulating each other as the kids blow plays or score on the field, offering each other some water, swapping stories about parenting, teachers, and homework drama. Before you know it, you've gone from complete strangers to athletic team supporters who have formed a friendly bond.

Yes, being social is a great thing, and so is feeling part of the community.

But since I'm here to help you become more aware of your personal surroundings and the threats they may unwittingly pose, it's important to realize that when you or your partner are having fun, meeting new people, laughing, and even sharing an activity as innocent as sitting on the sidelines of your kid's game, bonds can form. More to the point, bonds can lead to the destruction of healthy boundaries. Do not be blind to the possibility that either you or your partner could fall victim to this temptation! Being aware of the potential for social inappropriateness can keep it from occurring, and keep your relationship protected.

Breeding Ground #4:
Blast from the Past—Your Ex
In this day and age, an ex is never far away

Emotional Sex Scenario:

"I am floored. My wife sent her ex-boyfriend pics of herself in her bikini that I took when we were on our vacation to Hawaii. She told her ex to add them to the photo collection they once had and to 'update' it. She also said how happy she is that they reconnected on Facebook, that she can't wait to see him again, that she will always love him, and will never erase him from her heart. I asked her why? She could only say 'I would NEVER cheat on you; I don't believe in closing my heart just because a relationship is over. I just want to continue by being friends.' What the hell?"

It used to be that when we broke up with a romantic partner or went through a divorce, we might never run into that person again, unless perhaps we shared in the raising of children. This made it easier to move on, and avoid the temptation to reconcile or just have a fling with someone who once made us feel so comfortable, loved, and cherished.

Yet again, with the advent of Facebook, Linkedin, Google search and other social media/business networking opportunities, an old flame might try to find us or simply 'pop up' in some social media group we joined.

Poof! They're back, and with just a few keystrokes, there they are, ready to play on the vulnerabilities of the current relationship by being there when someone else cannot be, perhaps a shoulder to cry

> *Did YOU know?*
> **The initial decision to be unfaithful is rarely rational**
> **Most people are surprised by their own behavior at the start of an affair**

on when needed or a connection to the past that might bring up happier memories than the present.

Then, there are all the real-life situations, such as high school reunions and wedding parties, where we are up-close and personal with a love from the past. The heart starts racing. The gaze lingers for a little too long. And those romantic memories come flooding back. It's like being transported by a time machine that suddenly thrusts us back into a chapter of our life when we felt younger, more carefree, and like the 'two of us' were the only people in the world.

Don't be fooled by the memories of the past.
They are just that — MEMORIES...

faded by time
cleaned up by the present
romanticized by the vulnerable

Emotional Sex Scenario:

Thirty-something Deborah is happily remarried, but still socializes with her ex. After all, they have children together and need to stay connected. In fact, they are both proud of how mature they are about remaining friends after their divorce. "We're staying friendly for the kids. It's healthy for them. Besides, he knows me better than anyone and always has my best interests at heart!" She swears that everything is on the "up-and-up" even though there are suggestive silences, eye gazing, and playful banter. Sometimes, her ex even touches her affectionately, but it's all harmless. Besides, she's married to someone else now! She still gets a kick out of those double entendres that slip so easily into the conversation. It actually gives her a little shiver, but it's not a big deal—he's her ex-husband. She'd never cheat on her current husband, that's for sure, and just because someone is an ex does not mean she has to end the playful communication. It's only natural that they have to text, talk, email and get together all the time to stay on top of their kids active schedules.

Hmm... All that romantic stuff is behind us, correct? Which means reconnecting with an ex is no big threat to the current relationship, right? Wrong answer! Listen up. An ex is someone with whom we shared love, intense emotions, and physical sensations. Since we clearly get along today, any past wrongs are currently forgiven, reasons for breaking up may be forgotten, and the brain may simply and lovingly be picking up where we left off.

Think of it this way—we used to do a lot of mouth-to-mouth and quite a bit more with our now ex. Just who do we suppose could possibly be more threatening to our current relationship than someone who was once loved, trusted and cherished with full on intimacy?

Note to self:
Feelings that were once there can rise up again.

Easily

EMOTIONAL SEX
With An Ex
CHECK IN:

How would you respond or feel if...

❓ You found out your partner had renewed intimacy with their ex?

❓ Your partner's ex said they now realize your partner was the "one who got away" and they want a second chance to get it right with your partner? Would you be shocked and appalled, or amused and flattered that you had captured the one they wanted?

❓ Your ex wanted to reconnect and you felt that it might lead to something inappropriate? Would you reconnect? Would you take the chance for old times' sake? Or, would you refuse the connection because you are aware of the dangers?

When it comes to seeing, communicating and hanging out with an ex, what kind of behavior do you expect from your partner (and yourself)?

B-AWARE #2: BRAIN CHEMISTRY

Is it Love or Dopamine?
Love Gives You a Natural (and Addicting) High

Emotional Sex Scenario:

"Incredible! I feel attractive again! Like I'm on top of the world - the way it was when I was the captain of the football team and every cheerleader wanted me. Even though I'm 45 and have been married for 20 years, this proves I've still got it. It's a good time, pure pleasure — FUN, plain and simple. Besides, it's not hurting anyone. I'm so much happier now. In fact, maybe I didn't even realize how unhappy I was until I met her. This is no big deal. It's just a little excitement that makes me feel great — makes me feel like a man. Doesn't feeling good about myself make me more attractive in general? Shouldn't it pull my partner closer; even HELP my relationship? Clearly, there's nothing wrong with it. I work hard, I deserve to feel this good."

When you meet someone and feel an attraction, you probably describe the sensation as 'instant chemistry,' a palpable pull towards each other. Guess what? You're right.

---

*All those tingly, exciting feelings are truly being caused by **chemistry**...*

*specifically, **chemicals** in your brain*

You become obsessed with thoughts of him (or her) and long for your next flirtation fix. You check email incessantly or find excuses to text the person, just so you can prompt a response and be back in the game.

You'll do almost anything to keep the feelings going. Sounds like an addict, doesn't it? Well, wake up and smell the (caffeinated) coffee, because **LOVE IS ADDICTING**. In fact, if you were a scientist, you'd know that love ignites the same part of the brain that cocaine does. Yes, cocaine. Pretty heady stuff, isn't it?

I know what you're thinking. The looping monologue in your head is likely insisting, "No way, I'm no drug addict. What's wrong with a little romance? I can stop contact any time." Maybe so. Probably not.

The feeling of lust and love is chemically based in the brain. As such, they can be as entrapping as hard drugs, and just as gripping an addiction to break.

Brain chemicals do more than make you feel good and attracted to someone. They can also distort your assessment of that individual. When you look through the chemical eyes of love, you weed out the negative and selectively focus on the positive attributes.

Your 'friend' becomes the most adorable, intelligent, stimulating, deep, kind, emotionally generous, intuitive, sensitive person you've ever met.

You might even be telling yourself (and those you confide in) that this person is your 'perfect match' or 'soul mate,' both of which are feel good labels that give you a sense of entitlement about your growing relationship with them. After all, who would deprive you of being with the one person on the planet who really gets and appreciates you?

Did YOU know?
**LOVE Chemicals -
Like Most Drugs...
Mess with Your Head**

At the same time, the picture of your real partner distorts negatively in equal measure. Suddenly, in your warped and self-serving view, they are cold, constricted, critical, unloving, boring and undesirable, when (in truth) they may be behaving no differently at all.

The more you vilify your real partner, the more you justify your growing attachment to this OTHER person.

Reality check: **EMOTIONAL SEX** is often not driven by a disliking of your partner, but by the addictive processes fueled by your brain's hormones and chemicals. Just remember that song **Addicted to Love** - truer lyrics were never sung:

*"Your lights are on,
But you're not home,
Your mind is not your own...
You're gonna have to face it,
You're **ADDICTED TO LOVE!**"*

Robert Palmer knew it and so should you: *You're Addicted to Love* — a forbidden kind of love, which often makes it all the sweeter. You tell yourself this love is special. It feels good. It feels right, at least on some levels. The last thing you want to do is give it up.

Each brain chemical contributes to what I call the **3 S's** of **EMOTIONAL SEX** chemistry:

Secrecy
Shared Intimacy
Sexual Energy

Let's look at each brain chemical, also known as a neurotransmitter, so you'll understand how humans are influenced by this gang of hormones.

In short, you're about to find out that love is all in your head.

We Have Transmission:
Naughty Brain Chemicals that get us 'All Shook Up'

Dopamine (Street name: Romantic Love) - I like to call this God's little neurotransmitter. You know how you feel when you're in love? You're exhilarated, full of marathon-enduring energy and consumed by thoughts of that one incredible person who, in reality, you barely know. Hello? That's not love, that's an often deceptive little neurotransmitter known as dopamine. I say "deceptive" because, in this case, dopamine can set you up big time for something that's just not good for you. For example, because it's triggered by things that are novel and exciting, dopamine can transform you into a risk taker leading to Secrecy (one of those dangerous S's) and making you vulnerable to emotional and physical affairs. It can also add to the lust that's part of Sexual Energy, making dopamine a two-time S offender.

Oxytocin (Street name: The Social Glue) - A mother's swift and total surge of bonding with her newborn baby is caused in large part, by the hormone oxytocin. Considered as Mother Nature's way of creating instant love between a mother and child, oxytocin also gets busy in romantic relationships, too. For women, it plays a particular role in prompting emotional connection, building trust and sharing innermost feelings. For this reason, oxytocin is more of a factor for women when they are seeking a soul mate and partner. Oxytocin is one of three brain chemicals that can lead to the S of Shared Intimacy because it acts as a bonding agent. Think of it as emotional glue. But men are not totally out of the oxytocin picture. It turns out that oxytocin (mixed with a little dopamine) plays a significant role in men's sexual arousal as well as being a hormone released during orgasm, which deepens the desire to attach and bond.

Testosterone (Street name: The Sex Driver) - While most people think of testosterone as 'the male hormone', women's bodies produce it too, and it can drastically raise their libido. Whether you're male or female, when testosterone surges, there's potential for trouble—big time. In fact, studies suggest high-testosterone people have more affairs and higher divorce rates than those with average testosterone levels. This can cast doubt when it appears that the perfect lover is seducing you — is it adoration or merely off-the-chart testosterone driving the lust?

Testosterone is also involved in **S**hared Intimacy because women, in particular, associate sexuality with intimacy. But testosterone is really all about sex drive, which puts it squarely in the territory of **S**exual Energy. The drive to have sex can catapult you from Platonic Friendship knee deep into an emotional and physical affair.

Phenethylamine or PEA (Street name: Speedy Love) - This chemical speeds up the flow of information between nerve cells and works together with other neurotransmitters to provide that 'rush' of feelings. It's known to give you energy and magnify your mood. Not surprisingly, you'll find phenethylamine most concentrated in the part of the brain associated with emotions. Meaning if you're attracted to someone, as you are in an emotional affair, that feeling of being in a good mood all the time is being helped along by PEA. In short, love truly makes one a PEA-brain.

Norepinephrine (Street name: Infatuation) - Like dopamine, this chemical is a lot like amphetamines — you know, 'speed'. It contributes to the rush of lust and love, and physically makes the heart beat faster. (And you thought it was your new love that made your heart go pitter patter).

Serotonin (Street name: The Calm & Crazy Maker) - Serotonin is a neurotransmitter known for calming us. In essence, serotonin helps you maintain calm that develops when you are reliably and securely IN love versus the manic high of first FALLING in love. However, when you are having **EMOTIONAL SEX,** serotonin can also be a serious trouble maker (when it gets a bit of help from dopamine to trigger obsessive-compulsive thought patterns). In this type of situation, serotonin goes into full crazy-making mode, infusing your mind with obsessive, racing thoughts and/or feelings of depression as your brain spin cycles its way through longing, guilt and desire. Serotonin is why your new lover keeps popping into your mind and won't leave, and why you idolize the virtues and overlook the flaws. It greatly contributes to the feeling of **S**hared Intimacy.

CHEMICALS *in the* **BRAIN** *can be deceptive...*

B-Aware

Passion! Sex! Narcotics! With all these natural chemicals stimulating various parts of your brain and body, it's no wonder you're tempted to do wild, crazy and risky things.

Combine them with being in a vulnerable state or situation, and you just may find these very brain chemicals driving you straight into the arms (or at least the online presence) of an emotional lover.

---

*A person can feel **wedded and attached** to one person,*
sexually attracted *to another,*
*& **emotionally bonded** to a third!*

Okay, so you survived the chemistry lesson. But now you may be thinking, "With so much going on in my brain, how can I be expected to exercise any control over myself when I meet someone new?"

Now that you know why your brain behaves like it does when you're in love, you can think more clearly about how to prevent an affair and start repairing and strengthening your primary relationship.

An affair feels like the
Viagra™
antidote to boredom

B-AWARE #3: BOREDOM

Predictability, Complacency, and Apathy

BOREDOM: Weariness and lethargy due to dullness, detachment, disinterest, disgust, distaste, doldrums, ennui, fatigue, flatness, indifference, irksomeness, jadedness, lack of interest, listlessness, monotony, sameness, tedium, tiresomeness, or unconcern.

Emotional Sex Scenario:

"I have been married for five years (together for eight years in total). We have two children (ages 1 and 3). My husband is a very kind and loving man, but our relationship became routine after having children. I felt like I was in a rut. Last year, I had a brief online and sexting 'affair' with Frank, one of my husband's co-workers. Although it was exciting and sensual, it never turned physical, and we ended our contact after I confessed to my husband (without ever revealing Frank's true identity). My husband was very hurt, but forgave me. However, I became obsessed with missing Frank and the 'high' I got from our online relationship. To satisfy that craving, I ended up having a one night stand with a man I met online, as well as having several online affairs with guys I met on Craigslist Personals. About six months ago, I reconnected with Frank and we began a physical affair. I almost got busted when my husband discovered an email exchange between us—I had left my email open. He blatantly asked me if anything had ever happened with Frank because his instincts were telling him that something was off. He noted that Frank and I seemed overly flirtatious with one another. I denied it profusely. I wanted to tell him the truth, but I had promised Frank that I'd never tell since it would jeopardize his professional relationship. So I kept the lie going, and even continued the affair. The affair continued until recently—Frank ended up feeling so guilty about it that he told his fiancée. She ended their relationship, and he ended up 'breaking up' with me. He blames me for 'ruining' his relationship. He asked me to never email/contact him again. I feel lonelier than ever."

General Apathy is Major Boredom

When the emotional and sexual connection between two people becomes tedious, complacent, familiar, ho hum, distracted, boring, lonely... it is very easy for a relationship, once ripe with potential, to turn into a static, unfulfilling partnership.

A 'mundane existence' can lead a man or woman to cheat on their spouse or partner

When people are bored, they naturally look for adventure. A bored partner might then meet someone new (at work, online, at a soccer match, at the grocery store) and experience the longed-for rush of adrenaline.

Cheating is one of the ways to obtain and continue that adrenaline rush.

An affair provides that notion of adventure and gives a 'high' and escape from an ordinary and boring life or marriage. It alleviates the boredom of a settled routine and shakes up the predictable grind of everyday life.

It's **not about wanting to get a divorce**, it's just that once we get too comfortable (aka bored), we look to get attention elsewhere and unwittingly get caught up in feelings of passion and exhilaration that come with engaging in an affair.

Having an affair (whether it be emotional, physical or cyber) often appears to temporarily fill in the gaps and give us EVERYTHING our relationship is NOT.

CHEATING HAPPENS Because...

⮕ It feels thrilling and sensually gratifying. (Think dopamine rush).

⮕ It adds an element of fun and excitement that was previously missing.

⮕ If it's not physical, it can be justified as totally harmless.

⮕ It's a perfect MATCH! There are natural, varied similarities — similar interests, hobbies, beliefs, creativity. It's as if you were made for each other.

⮕ You don't have to look for 'openers' with this person. You can chat — in person, or through instant messaging - for hours with this person, and it feel like mere minutes.

⮕ It just FLOWS. Conversation is so easy. It's effortless to open up and be heard.

⮕ It FEELS OLD and NEW at the same time. You've found a person who feels like a soul mate; your mirror image, someone who you feel like you've known forever.

⮕ Even though there is no 'sexual' component, no consummation, your emotional confidant makes you feel incredibly sexy. They light your fire, yet you've never been 'burned'.

⮕ You suddenly feel young, attractive and desirable again. You are flattered, basking in the glow of newfound emotions. They bring the heat — to your heart and your loins — both areas that may have gone cold with your partner's indifference or complacency.

⮕ Anything sexual—be it SEXting, video chatting while touching yourself sexually, watching pornography, fantasizing while making love with your partner, enjoying lap dances in strip joints or getting bonus massages in massage parlors—is equal to masturbation and thus, doesn't really count as 'cheating'.

⮕ Since there is no physical involvement (or at least not yet), you feel assured that there's not the slimmest chance of ever being caught.

⮕ After all, your affair is not hurting anyone, and you're not having REAL sex, so why not?

Affair B-AWARE
Dissatisfaction Downward Spiral

We get so busy that we forget to give each other the **ATTENTION**, **APPRECIATION** and **AFFECTION** our relationship requires.

Communication breaks down.

An **emotional distance** sets in and then a physical distance follows.

We **sail apart** as we focus on our own thing and before we know it, we are living separate lives.

We take each other for granted, **complacency** takes over and we forget that our love will not take care of itself.

Our primary relationship is **no longer a source of nurturance**, joy and well-being.

When one partner starts complaining, *"I'm starving"* and the other doesn't hear the call, the dissatisfaction rises, the need for attention increases and this results in one or both partners seeking **EMOTIONAL SEX** with another.

It's easy to get that attention you want and need elsewhere.

Boredom *leads to a need for something new something new leads to an affair*

MEN AND WOMEN STATS & FACTS[†]

Did YOU know?

1. A **lack of sexual excitement,** or the routine of having sex with the same person, often **leads men to stray.**

2. When having a one-night stand, **men are less choosy than women** when it comes to selecting someone to have sex with.

3. Husbands are more likely to feel that **cheating is justified** due to the lack of sex within a marriage.

4. When a wife does cheat on her husband, **she is more likely to have an emotional affair.**

5. Women are less likely than men to have a **one-night stand.**

6. When women cheat, they are also more likely to view their infidelity as a **symptom of the problems** in their relationship.

7. By comparison, **men have an easier time separating** infidelity from the problems they face at home.

Did YOU know? A relationship will STARVE if two people are not regularly feeding it with **ATTENTION, APPRECIATION & AFFECTION**

[†] adapted from: http://www.truthaboutdeception.com/cheating_spouse/public/cheating_wife.html

CHAPTER

3

AFFAIR AWARE

DETECTION

Cyber, Emotional, Physical,
Or All Three

THE 3 S's OF EMOTIONAL SEX CHEMISTRY

Heed the **RED FLAGS**

DETECTION CHECK POINT
for emotional, cyber and physical affairs

Is it time to heed the **Red Flags?**

Does your partner seem to be...

- Less present, available, or eager to be around you?
- Generally less interested in you and your life together?
- Moody (e.g. happy and energetic when leaving the house or with friends; down, depressed or bored when with you)?
- Quick to become annoyed, frustrated, disenchanted or unhappy?
- Expressing doubts or concerns about love and/or your relationship?
- So far-away, that you feel like you can't get close?
- Evasive or defensive about outside activities?
- Unwilling to talk about a future with you or make future plans?
- Avoiding getting into serious discussions or confrontation at all costs?
- More discontented, blaming, picking fights or argumentative?
- Withholding their feelings and/or have little regard for yours?
- Emotionally distant, avoiding, ignoring, or being dismissive of you?
- To be MIA for spells - hard to get a hold of with no explanation for absences?

* If you answered YES to any of the above, then...

... *it's time to become* **AFFAIR AWARE**

Emotional Sex Scenario:

"I had every reason to worry, but chose to think otherwise. It is very hard for people of the opposite sex to be in a close relationship without crossing the boundaries, especially, if you know the potential for attraction is there. If the other man/woman is a former flame or love interest, you KNOW the attraction is there. Do not ignore the signs. I am recently separated from my wife who was having an affair. At first, I ignored the signs and, in a way, enabled it to continue. If you suspect your partner of cheating, confront them and say how it makes you feel. Trust your gut and share your feelings. If your feelings are disrespected or downplayed, your partner does not have you or the best interests of your relationship at heart. I learned this lesson through personal experience and self-denial."

The **3 S's** that feed chemistry and keep a relationship connection exciting are - **Secrecy, Shared Intimacy, and Sexual Energy**. These qualities energize our chemistry and help us feel up close and personal with one another. Secrecy gives us the sense that the relationship is private, sacred, and just between us. Sharing Intimacy builds trust, closeness and deep companionship with one another. Sexual energy makes us feel that our bond is special, personal, and on a different and more uniquely physical level than a non-romantic (platonic) friendship.

Most people feel the **3 S's should be reserved exclusively** for their primary relationship, and often feel betrayed if they are shared with anyone else.

Shifts in any of the **3 S's** are red flags that it's time to become affair aware.

"S" #1: SECRECY

When there is a platonic friendship, both partners can join in. Nobody is *excluded*. The friendship is open and talked about, clear and well-intentioned. There is nothing to hide, lie or feel guilty about because there is no inappropriateness to the relationship.

The moment secrecy and deception are introduced into your relationship, emotional distance will grow. If your partner is keeping secrets, telling lies (even innocent ones), then the intimacy between the two of you will begin to erode. The bigger the secret, the more emotional distance it creates. The more there is to hide, the bigger the emotional chasm between you.

 Is your partner being secretive?

❓ Is your partner now locking up or password protecting their computer, phone or personal accounts and not allowing you access?

❓ Is your partner getting really defensive or secretive about his or her stuff, time, or friendships?

❓ Is your partner keeping meetings, messaging, and conversations on the sly?

❓ Is there a change in your partner's habits, routines or attitudes?

❓ Does your partner snap at you for being "too nosy"?

❓ Do you have a gut feeling that something isn't right?

RED FLAG BEHAVIORS for SECRECY

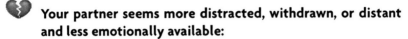

Your partner seems more distracted, withdrawn, or distant and less emotionally available:

There is less intimacy, sharing, talking, and self-disclosures. Your partner has been acting emotionally distant and withdrawn but when you ask about it, they don't want to discuss it and become very protective of their privacy.

Your partner wants more space, privacy, autonomy and time to him or herself:

They want to do their own thing more often and become indifferent to doing things together and offer excuses about not planning or committing to future trips, vacations, and family visits.

Your partner doesn't share much about their day and when asked about what they're doing, gets evasive, defensive or offensive:

Your mate becomes easily offended when you make normal and natural inquiries and may demand to know why you are "checking up" on them. They may also put you on the defensive acting as if you're crazy, paranoid, or irrational.

Your partner seems to be spending increased periods on the computer, texting or talking on the phone:

Your partner may 'stiffen' when you enter the room, or put the phone away suddenly. They may have increased activity or text messaging but are more difficult to get a hold of when out of the house.

Your partner secures their files and folders on the computer with passwords:

Your partner has Facebook, email and social media accounts that you don't have access to even though you share bank accounts and other personal passwords.

Your partner gets defensive or evasive when questioned about his/her friendship with another:

They offer short, sharp responses when you ask them seemingly simple questions about their 'friend' or associate, or they over-explain when there is no need and their stories don't quite add up.

"S" #2: SHARED INTIMACY

While it's important for everyone to have a strong support system to bolster them in life, there is a marked difference between platonic friendship and **EMOTIONAL SEX**. When one or both partners are drawn to another person outside of their relationship because they share interests, hobbies, work commitments or similar life experiences, the new person may open up doors of excitement or attraction that leads to the desire to get close, be known, and spend more and more time together.

Is your partner giving time, attention and affection to another?

❓ Is your partner beginning to isolate from you, no longer desiring to talk intimately, share with you, know you, or be known by you?

❓ Does your partner put their friend first, and make excuses for not being able to be there for you?

❓ Do you have any REAL idea of how much time they are spending together?

❓ Does it feel like more is going on than is being revealed?

❓ Is there a shift for no apparent reason in how your partner is treating you (i.e. more critical, grouchy, disinterested, bored or conversely extra nice)?

❓ Does your partner seem to be distracted? Do they seem to space out when you're talking to him/her or doesn't seem to be paying attention to your concerns?

RED FLAG BEHAVIORS for SHARING INTIMACY

Your partner gets overcritical about your appearance and behavior:

Criticizing things about you that he or she once found attractive and appealing.

Your partner easily becomes offended at the comments, however harmless, that you make:

Seems more willing to pick fights, arguments, and conflicts.

Your partner is spending more time outside the house and your relationship than he/she usually does:

There are sudden or erratic changes in work schedule, habits, hobbies, time away, texting, or on the internet.

Your partner starts paying less attention to you, your children and home-life in general:

It feels like your partner is giving more time, attention and emotional support to their online friend, co-worker/work, sports, _____(fill in the blank) than you and the family. You sense an emotional distance growing between you - less intimacy, sharing, talking and self-disclosure. The love between you feels more hollow.

There may be an increased reference or talking about the third party:

They may talk about their 'friend' a lot in glorious terms. May spark conversations asking you something along the lines of... "Do you believe that it's possible to love more than one person at a time?" Conversely, they may never mention that person and even close down if the name comes up.

When you fight or argue, your partner's fallback position is about your relationship ending:

"What would you do if our relationship ended?" or "I can't take this anymore" or even "If anything ever happened to us, I would always love you like a friend." In general, they seem overtly negative about your relationship.

"S" #3: SEXUAL ENERGY

A platonic friendship is an open friendship that everyone knows about and that generates no special thrill... Platonic friendships do not have the elements of sexual chemistry or attraction. In fact, sexual thoughts with a platonic friend feels incestuous. With **EMOTIONAL SEX** there is a strong, palpable sexual attraction and chemistry (forbidden sex) pulsating between the two people, whether admitted or not. They look for reasons to be together, touch each other, and usually harbor sexual fantasies about wanting to make love and more. This sexual energy being generated and energized outside of the primary relationship may strongly impact the exchange of affection, contact, and sexual availability of the primary partners.

What kind of sexual energy is being exchanged in your relationship?

❓ Is there a change in affection and sexual contact between you and your partner?

❓ Does your partner's desire to be 'attractive' seem to have increased?

❓ Is your partner more interested in reading a book or watching television than talking with you or making love to you?

❓ When you do make love, is your partner present or do they seem to be far way and fantasizing?

❓ Is your partner becoming more outwardly flirtatious with others?

❓ Is your partner running hot and cold when it comes to sex?

RED FLAG BEHAVIORS for SEXUAL ENERGY

 Your partner is changing how they look and dress when leaving the house:

Sudden changes in clothing, appearance, or interest in getting in shape. May try to fix perceived insecurities by losing weight, working out, buying new clothes, changing hair, applying makeup more often. Might even have a change of clothes in the car or in a sports bag that doesn't fit going to the gym or simply hanging out with friends.

 Your partner's sexual interest, level of contact and passion is different:

May feel like your partner is going through the motions, or seems less available, affectionate or intimate with you. Conversely, your partner is suddenly more sexual, may want to try something new, or may appear to be fantasizing more during sex or calls out another name. Perhaps it doesn't feel like your partner is making love to you anymore.

 Your gut is picking up that there may be an attraction between your partner and their 'friend':

Your partner is changing the way they act whenever the other person is around (i.e. much more conversational, animated, interested) similar to who they were with you when you started dating. Conversely, your mate may criticize this other person trying to make you think that type of individual would never be of interest to them. You will notice attention (positive or negative) flowing away from you towards another.

 *Does your relationship feel different to you?*

❓ Is there more distance in your relationship?

❓ Does your partner seem to be sneaking around, hiding stuff, changing passwords on the computer, or becoming more secretive?

❓ Is there increased interest in their cell phone or the Internet?

❓ Do you feel unusually jealous or insecure but don't have any clue why?

❓ Are you suddenly asking yourself, "Hey, where did the love go?"

THESE ARE THE RED FLAGS THAT OUGHT TO MAKE YOU SIT UP AND REALIZE THAT SOMETHING IS NOT RIGHT IN THE HEARTLAND

Did
YOU know?
Your gut instinct is designed to protect you
Listen *to it*

Emotional Sex Scenario:

I travel a lot on business. After returning from my last trip, I was shocked – but initially pleased – when my wife initiated a fantastic night of adventurous lovemaking. It was totally out of character for her and puzzled me, but I figured I'd roll with it. After being intimate, she got up to use the bathroom, and her phone buzzed with a text message on the nightstand beside me. A quick glance at it confirmed my fears: It read "I miss you, sexy," and in that brief instant I knew there was someone else in her life. Sometimes, I'll wake up in the middle of the night when she gets out of bed and see the light from her cell phone in the bathroom – and I know who she's texting. I know what my wife is doing, but I don't how to prove it"

CHAPTER

4

CATCHING THEM
IN THE ACT

You Suspect Your Loved One
Is Cheating And Now You Are
Ready To Find Out

PUTTING IT ALL TOGETHER

REAL *CLUES AND CUES*
you should look for..

First a disclaimer and a heads up: While this entire section provides you with many of the **EMOTIONAL SEX** warning signs to be aware of and guides you in what to do once you recognize the clues, I urge you to proceed with caution. Just because your loved one might display a few or many of these secretive and suspicious behaviors does NOT mean they are necessarily **CHEATING** on you. It could be any number of reasons outside of **CHEATING** that they haven't yet told you about, be it a problem at work, with family, their health, etc... Keeping secrets from each other, withdrawing, and withholding important communication of any kind can lead to you feeling the same kind of emotional disconnect, fearfulness and mistrust as **CHEATING**.

Here are some **HUGE, MEGA, TRUMPET BLARING Cyber and Physical CLUES AND CUES** that your partner may be having an affair:

- ➡ Work hours and *other* commitments seem to have expanded.
- ➡ An increase in attending out of town meetings, conferences, conventions or classes.
- ➡ Odd behavior – i.e. coming home after work or an evening out and taking a shower before coming to bed.
- ➡ Your partner has email addresses and web site accounts that you don't have access to.
- ➡ Your partner gets edgy or defensive when you get near the computer or ask too many questions about what's going on.
- ➡ When you walk into the room, there is a sudden change in their behavior or activity such as clicking or closing of screens.

- Your Internet browsing history is filled with inappropriate searches or obvious gaps in browser history.

- Your partner is spending more time on the computer or phone – talking, texting, browsing and messaging.

- Your partner receives regular texts from a 'friend' you don't know or didn't know your partner had.

- Your partner is taking mysterious calls in the other room and clearly doesn't want you to hear the conversation. When you ask who called, they say, "No one," "Wrong number," "It's business," or "Why do you ask?"

- Your partner is hiding the communications received or sent.

- Their recent call list is continually being deleted.

- Your partner is distant, distracted, or disinterested when they come off the computer.

- Your partner's computer time is impacting the amount of time they have available to spend with you.

- Your partner's sexual appetite and desire for you is changing.

- Your partner is running more and more errands away from the house.

- You are noticing inconsistencies between what is being said and how your partner's time and money is REALLY being shared and spent.

- Your partner is withdrawing from normal activities, household duties or social plans.

The attempt to hide/avoid/distract/lie are all signals that your partner could be 'checking out' from the real life you have together and 'checking into' a fantasy world that involves someone else.

WHAT IS YOUR PARTNER TRYING TO HIDE — AND WHY?

GATHERING THE EVIDENCE

From suspicion to **REAL** Proof...

DO NOT make random accusations!

Find concrete proof-positive evidence BEFORE you CONFRONT your partner.

Be warned – Do NOT do anything illegal. Make sure that you are not leaving yourself exposed in a legal sense, and be sure that you have an open and closed case. Electronic snooping, however, is a whole different playing field that's regulated by both State and Federal Law. The easiest ways to find out whether a partner is cheating are usually NOT legal. What type of activities could land a snooping partner in jail? Using a password to illegally snoop through personal email files. In most states, email is considered private conversation, subject to 'reasonable expectations' that what is written between parties on email is protected, even in the case of a husband and wife. The *Orlando Sentinel* reported that a spurned Michigan spouse is learning the hard way. The husband is a computer professional, and when signs arose that his wife was cheating, he accessed her email to find evidence. Unfortunately for him, he now faces felony charges that could land him in prison for up to five years. Likewise, accessing any private computer account – like Facebook – is illegal.

It is important to remain calm, cool and collected and not rush to confront prematurely at the first suspicious evidence you discover. Be super, extra cautious not to get caught snooping, and be sure to have a good story in place if you do. Otherwise, you'll be the one put in the hot seat and accused of being a jealous, crazy, distrusting lunatic. Suddenly, it will be about YOU and not your partner's actions.

There is always a 'paper trail' associated with **EMOTIONAL SEX**, so look for it–phones, computers and other electronic devices; briefcases, drawers or personal storage spaces; office areas, desks and even cars can also hold many secrets. Do not forget to look in his or her pockets, purses or wallet for receipts, love notes or even hotel stays.

✅ Check the contacts and calls on their cell phone.

Who are they really talking to?

- View contact lists, call history and photo library. Read text messages. View the calendar and appointments. Take a photo of anything suspicious.

- Check out suspicious names or numbers you don't recognize that have been called repeatedly (especially during personal hours, after you've gone to bed, or during a time out of contact with you).

- A big sign of something fishy going on behind your back is if you come to learn that one of the numbers listed in your partner's phone is actually a fake name (hint: There are sites that do a reverse phone look up).

- Upload and save their 'friendly photos' of another to your computer.

- Look for apps such as TigerText (named after Tiger Woods) which deletes texts upon reading and enables private chatting and sexting.

- Don't have access to the cell phone? Then find the phone bill – paper version or online – and view the calls made and received.

✅ Check out credit card charges.

Where's the money going?

- Check their pockets, wallet, desk or waste basket for bills and receipts.

- Look at the bank accounts for unexplained expenditures, questionable purchases and cash withdrawals.

- Explore the credit card statements and look for purchases to events, concerts, movies, or dinners that you have either never heard of or been invited to.

- Look for restaurant receipts that reflect dinner for two when your partner said they were alone or with a group.
- Look for purchases of intimate clothing articles (not shared with you), gifts or increased shopping activity.
- Check out the closet for new clothing purchases that your partner showed no previous interest in wearing.

✓ What does their calendar say?
Check Outlook, Google Calendars or a physical calendar to see if there are inconsistencies between where they said they have been and what the receipts actually show.

✓ Does your partner smell or taste different?

✓ Check their car for tell-tale signs of an affair.
If you don't have a key, call a locksmith and make an extra key. Check the glove compartment, trunk, as well as under and between the seats. Look for anything different– articles of clothing or items that don't belong to you or your partner; a suitcase with necessary incidentals; a gym bag that hasn't been to the gym; condoms; and dated receipts. Photograph the evidence.

✓ Write down dates and times that your partner's behavior is suspicious or inconsistent.
If you have the means and the inclination, you might want to Google 'infidelity surveillance' to see what else you can do or who else you can hire to help you. This search will help you find everything from hiring private investigators to installing spyware on your partner's phone and computer.

45-55%
of married women and
50-60%
of married men
engage in extramarital sex at
some time or another during
their relationship [1]

70% *of married*
women and **54%** *of*
married men
did not know of their
spouses' extramarital
activity [2]

23% *of Men are*
more likely to cheat with
someone they met at a bar

22% *of Women are more*
drawn to old flames [3]

1   Atwood & Schwartz, 2002 - Journal of Couple & Relationship Therapy
2   Associated Press
3   Your unadulterated thoughts on adultery: The lowdown on the MSNBC.com/iVillage Lust, Love & Loyalty survey
     4/16/2007   http://www.msnbc.msn.com/id/18055526/ns/health-sexual_health/t/your-unadulterated-thoughts-
     adultery/

... What are you waiting for?

CHAPTER

5

CONFRONTATION

My partner IS cheating on me!
Now what?

*How to talk about the details,
get the truth, and find out
why the affair happened.*

WHEN CONFRONTING YOUR PARTNER THE IDEAL OUTCOME IS:

CONFRONTATION ➔ CONVERSATION ➔ CONFESSION

➔ which leads to an **ILLUMINATION**

But (as I mentioned earlier):
EVIDENCE IS THE ESSENCE

Before you even consider confronting your partner, it is essential that you have proof – not a hunch, an idea or a fear, but REAL, TANGIBLE proof.

If you suspect your partner is having a cyber, emotional or physical affair, don't make accusations until you have **concrete evidence** to make your case and get a *confession*.

*After all, a confession is what you're after. Once you have a **confession** you can work at a **solution**.*

To confront your partner, you must have proof of the infidelity, such as text, email, or voicemail messages; a private detective's report; a piece of clothing you found that doesn't belong to you; even a recorded phone call or photographs—something that you can produce as evidence of the infidelity, as a non-negotiable and undeniable 'check mate'.

Without proof you will look like a distrusting fool at best and, at worst, you will ensure that your cheating partner learns to better cover their tracks.

PROOF is your ally.

PROOF is the essential ingredient you must acquire *before* the **CONFRONTATION.**

Only when you have PROOF can you proceed.

Emotional Sex Scenario:

"I discovered numerous text messages and saved voice messages on my husband's cell phone from his "friend" who is a girl half his age! I've given him articles on the dangers of emotional affairs, but it only made him angry. He refuses to read them, saying they have nothing to do with him and that I should not get upset because he and his "friend" have never had sex. Well, we're not having sex either! I know that he's hiding what he is doing and how often he feels the need to communicate with her. I'm very upset. At this point, I just want to know the truth, whether it hurts us or not. What should I do?"

If you see signs of **INFIDELITY**, the most important thing to do is **remain calm**.

Remaining calm, cool, and collected will be the deciding factor in your success or failure in confronting your partner and getting to the truth.

As the saying goes,
the truth will set you free...

But how do you remain calm during this devastating time?

✅ By seeing the bigger picture, by stepping back and making sure you have the necessary proof, by collecting evidence of the affair AND by preventing your partner from knowing you're on to them, you will enable yourself to acquire the proof needed to confront them.

✅ By keeping yourself in balance, busy, and focused on other activities (especially ones that bring you pleasure), you will be in a more receptive and calmer state to find out the truth (or at least as much as you can handle).

When confronting your partner, be sure that you are emotionally prepared for the outcome of the conversation.

THINK **CALM,** BE **CALM**

Connect in, Center and Breathe. Quiet down until still.

Assess what's happening in your body, mind and heart. What's tight, tense, scared or reactive?

Listen deeply to your body's call and send loving **attention** through your breath to the tension. As you breathe, imagine the tension softening, relaxing or flowing away.

Mindfully Meditate. As you inhale, inwardly say the word PEACE to yourself, and as you exhale, say the word CALM. Draw out the punctuation of the word so that it lasts for the entire breath. p-e-e-a-a-a-c-c-c-e-e-e as you inhale... c-a-a-a-l-l-l-m-m-m-m-m-m as you exhale. Continue until you feel very relaxed and calm.

CALM - Absence of agitation; tranquility; serenity; peace; without rough motion; still or nearly still; not windy or stormy; an unruffled state, especially under disturbing conditions.

While you are taking these deep breaths, affirm to yourself

I feel calm.
I am safe.
I can handle this.

I am CALM. I am READY. I want the secretiveness to stop.

GETTING TO THE TRUTH

First the ⊗ Don'ts and then the ✓ DO'S

⊗ DON'T:

DON'T irritate the cheater

⊗ DON'T be combative:

- ➲ Approaching this as a confrontation will only cause your partner to react defensively; they will withdraw, counter attack, become hostile and deny.
- ➲ Being combative will do you no favors. Name calling, accusing, or attacking will only be counter-productive.
- ➲ Being combative will not help you get to the truth.

⊗ DON'T share all your evidence, and DON'T reveal your sources:

- ➲ Most cheaters will try to concoct a story to fit the evidence presented rather than spill the truth.
- ➲ Strategically withhold evidence.
- ➲ Only present evidence that counters their story. This will cause them to question exactly how much you know and how you learned about it.
- ➲ Most importantly, it will encourage them to come clean and tell the truth.

✖ DON'T contact the other party:

➡ Often it is easier to blame the other party than it is to blame your partner. You might even want to confront them – DON'T.

➡ Contacting the other party will only confuse the situation even more.

➡ Contacting the other party will only anger your partner more.

➡ This is an issue between you and your partner, not you and the other party.

✖ DON'T be surprised, and DON'T lose your cool:

➡ Be prepared that your partner may at first get defensive, offensive, or deny and counter everything you say, show or present.

➡ Be prepared to persevere.

DO:

DO persevere to get to the truth.

Make sure you have the 4 P's covered:

Proof, Preparation, Plan & Purpose

✅ Proof:

- ➡ Present your hard evidence to punch through any denial.

✅ Preparation:

- ➡ Be prepared for escape clauses and dismissal of your accusations so you can counter any arguments (i.e. "It's just a special friendship.", "No sex is involved.", "You're crazy!" etc.).
- ➡ Make sure you are emotionally ready - practice being CALM.

✅ Plan:

- ➡ Make a plan to confront your partner and discuss the affair without any interruption.
- ➡ Choose the time and place carefully, then present the evidence a piece at a time.

✅ Purpose:

- ➡ Know that your purpose is to get the truth.
- ➡ Listen carefully to your partner's answers so you can accurately assess the situation.

This is an ongoing discussion;
everyone needs to come out of the
shock and denial first

THINK CONVERSATION NOT CONFRONTATION

The conversation is the essence to reaching ILLUMINATION

These are the best ways to proceed:

✅ **Stay Calm** - be cool, composed, collected

- ➲ As I mentioned earlier, it is very important to remain calm, no matter how much you may want to inflict physical harm on your cheating partner!
- ➲ Approach your partner in a rational, non-threatening way.
- ➲ Stay calm and remain focused on getting to the truth.
- ➲ At first, your partner may resist the wake up call, and may not want to step out of the **EMOTIONAL SEX** haze.
- ➲ Give it time and your calm approach will break down their barriers.

Keep affirming to yourself...

I feel calm.

I am safe.

I can handle this

✅ Conversation - be conversational

- ➲ Use this **conversation** as a way to come **TOGETHER** to resolve your problems.

- ➲ Allow the conversation to develop into a discussion that helps you **BOTH** understand what went wrong and what you can do about it now.

✅ Limit the Questions - be diplomatic

- ➲ Studies show that cheaters shut down and lie when asked too many pointed questions: *Who were you with? Why did you lie? How could you do this to me?* These are the kind of questions that will get your partner to withhold the truth, become defensive, and clam up because they feel scared, trapped, and cornered.

- ➲ The answer is to talk about yourself first. Focus on your feelings and start each sentence with "I" not "you." This will help your partner soften and be less reactive.

- ➲ Try to phrase the problem in the least judgmental way possible by starting off with, *"Something I discovered is upsetting me. I'm concerned (sad, hurt, frustrated) about... and I want to be able to talk with you about it..."* This will maximize your chances of being heard and getting the truth about the affair out in the open.

✅ Apply The OREO COOKIE

POSITIVE - THE PROBLEM - POSITIVE

- ⊙ Approach your partner with something POSITIVE, state THE PROBLEM, close with something POSITIVE.

- ⊙ **The chocolate** (POSITIVE) - Start with: *"I love you. I'm devastated. I need to talk to you about this. I want to hear the truth. I want to understand and work this out."*

- ⊙ **The filling** (THE PROBLEM) - Show your partner the evidence: *"This is what I believe. This is what I know. This is what I'm concerned about. This is how it makes me feel."*

- ⊙ **The chocolate** (POSITIVE) - Complete the Oreo Cookie with the positive: *"I want us to work this out. I want to save our relationship. I want to get to the truth, so we can work through this. I'm not sure how we're going to get through this, but that's what I want, and this is what I need from you to get there."*

Although it is immensely difficult, when you confront your partner, the best thing to do is to come from a place of love— that is the essence of The Oreo Cookie (we all love an Oreo Cookie, right?)

Love is the most effective tool for getting at the truth.

The benefit of using the Oreo Cookie approach is that if you can create a sense of understanding and a willingness to discuss problems without a lot of negativity, you and your partner will feel more comfortable discussing issues in the future.

Your partner will probably be in shock and denial. But no matter what your partner says or does, you MUST persevere.

To get to the TRUTH, keep insisting: *"I love you. I want our relationship to work. This has got to stop. This is what I need."*

CONFESSION... OR MAYBE NOT

What to do if your Partner
Deceives, Denies, Distracts or Defends

Emotional Sex Scenario:

"My partner is cheating! I have the positive proof (i.e. texts, emails, and a recorded call between them). When I ask him, he refuses to talk about it. How can I get him to address my concerns and confess?"

Emotional Sex Scenario:

"I confronted my husband yesterday about his inappropriate "friendship" with Vicky, a woman he works with. Lately, his cell phone seems to be attached to his body - he's using it 24/7, making and receiving nonstop phone calls and texts. Usually he leaves the room. Plus, he began to hide his phone and clear the data right away. My husband is home less than before and stays out late, claiming he has to work. What is he thinking? Does he have no clue how much his behavior hurts me? I feel utterly betrayed, yet he says I'm nuts for even thinking that he's having an affair or that anything he's doing is out of the ordinary. He swears up and down that Vicky is a co-worker, that's all. He finally agreed to stop communicating with her outside of work because he loves me. That's certainly a start but they see each other every day at the office. How can I be sure that he is telling me the truth?"

B-AWARE *AVOIDANCE TACTICS*

DECEPTION - DENIAL - DISTRACTION - DEFENSE

When it comes to **physical infidelity**, the lines that have been crossed are so obvious and damaging that the cheater will do everything they can to lie about and hide the betrayal in order to maintain the status quo and avoid the severe consequences that will come when you know of their actions. When confronted, your partner may **deny**, **distract** and **deceive** either to *protect* themselves or *protect* you from the pain of knowing. They may fear the subsequent emotional fallout and want to avoid the inevitable changes that lie ahead.

When it comes **emotional and cyber infidelity,** the boundaries are blurred and open to interpretation, so recognizing that the lines of infidelity have been crossed is not as clear-cut as physical infidelity (where there is a tangible offense). It is often easy for the emotional betrayer to deceive themselves (and you) into thinking their behavior is *meaningless* and *harmless*. Because there has been no sexual infidelity, your partner will be convinced of his/her innocence and their denial may be even more defensive or aggressive.

So, don't be surprised if your partner gets **defensive,** adamantly **denying** any and all wrongdoing and dismissing everything you claim. They may use the **DISTRACTION tactic** to turn the tables and attack YOU calling you paranoid or crazy, shaming you for snooping and being distrustful.

They may even blame you for the fact they were spending time with someone else, saying the other person was just being a supportive friend because YOU were dropping the ball in the relationship by not providing something your partner needs or wants.

Be prepared for denial, distraction, defensiveness, and deception which are very common when partners are first confronted with *evidence* of an affair.

WHY DO CHEATERS LIE ABOUT THEIR BEHAVIOR AND DENY THEY ARE IN THE WRONG?

Typically, deceptive behavior is driven by one of our most basic emotions: FEAR – the fear of being embarrassed, punished, abandoned or rejected. Your partner may lie as a passive or indirect way of getting you to 'back off ' or 'let it be.'

This is another reason for confronting your partner in a way that is calm and gentle.

When you approach things in a way that alleviates fear, people are more likely to respond in a way that is forthright and honest.

Partners lie about having an affair to avoid:

- ◑ Facing the truth about their behavior to themselves.
- ◑ Hurting you.
- ◑ An argument or confrontation.
- ◑ Confessing.
- ◑ You taking control of the situation by leaving or making them change.
- ◑ Having to tell the painful truth.
- ◑ Losing respect, love, security and family.

Here are some of the ways your partner may lie to you:

- ◑ By making misleading statements and/or concealing the truth.
- ◑ By leaning towards you and pretending nothing is wrong.
- ◑ By looking at you like you're crazy.
- ◑ Through actions, gestures or silences that tacitly support a lie or false assumption.

- By telling a half truth (e.g., leaving out important information or details).
- By presenting false information, adamantly asserting that it is true.

Keep your **eyes open** for signs that they are lying. Often, it's not what you hear, but what you see and feel that says it all.

Your partner's **body language** will tell you as much as their words. Note unusual changes from their normal behavior.

Research suggests that lying people may:

- offer shorter, curt, evasive responses.
- make more vocalizations between words – more um's, er's, ah's.
- blink more.
- lick their lips more. (When we get nervous, our saliva glands stop producing saliva and our mouths become dry. People lick their lips more when they are nervous, or are uncomfortable about what is being said.)
- fidget and squirm more.
- place objects between you and themselves (cups, utensils, pillows, chairs, etc.) as an unconscious barrier.
- make gestures that don't match their words. (say 'I love you' but look angry. Say 'no' but shake head yes).

Did YOU know?
People often
LIE or DENY
when accused of
infidelity

Both men and women who have betrayed someone use the same justifications:

- "It's non-sexual."
- "I'm under a lot of stress."
- "It doesn't mean anything."
- "I'm not doing anything wrong."
- "You're crazy!"
- "You weren't meeting my needs."
- "Lighten up. It was just a text. It's totally harmless and meaningless."

PUSHING FOR THE TRUTH

When we love and want to trust someone, it can create huge blind spots in our ability to see and hear the truth.

No one wants to believe a partner is lying to them, especially when the subject is infidelity. Which is why, with our hopeful mindset

it is far easier to accept a *pleasant lie*
than to acknowledge a *devastating truth*

You MUST keep pressing for the truth:

Keep asking your partner for what you want.

Keep telling yourself, "*I'm in charge here and I'm going to get to the bottom of this, using love!*" This is especially true if you have a lot of hard evidence of the affair.

The more proof you possess and the more you already know, the greater the chance you'll have to get your partner to come clean.

If you can do it with love and an expressed desire to use the confession for good – to ultimately improve your relationship – the conversation will be far more fruitful.

Don't get me wrong, there is absolutely a need–and it's a healthy one–to vent and release your pain and anger. In fact, it is essential to your own healing as well as the healing of your relationship that you are able to express your emotions. I will cover this extensively later in the book.

SECURING THE CONFESSION
notes to myself

The more calmly you deal with the truth, the more people will tell you the truth.

As a general rule, people are more likely to be candid and forthcoming with you if you seem to understand where they are coming from—why they were motivated to do something, and what reward they felt for doing it.

Conversely, the more poorly you react when told the truth (e.g., pouting, sulking, crying, shouting, flying off the handle) the more your partner will feel punished for being honest—and the more they will either lie or shut down.

Remember that getting to the truth is the golden ticket when confronting your partner. While hearing them admit that they have cheated will hurt you to the core, the truth is also the doorway to a better and healthier relationship.

Chances are, you will become upset by what you hear—and it is entirely normal and healthy that you do. It's okay to let your partner know how you feel in the moment, provided it's not done in a way that is attacking or intentionally hurtful.

Telling someone that you are upset by what happened, without reacting poorly, is hard but it does lead to more truthful exchanges in the long run and in the short term.

GET STABILIZED
BREATHE - CENTER- CALM

ILLUMINATION

As your partner admits the TRUTH of their infidelity, you may be inundated with millions of questions you want to ask about the *what, where, how, when,* and *whys* of the CHEATING. Rarely does the cheater reveal the width and depth of their indiscretions all at once. And, in truth, you may not be **ready** to hear ALL the sordid details. It's too much painful information to process at one time. Even if you've known or suspected the truth for a while, validation of the truth shakes everything to the core. I advise you to take your time. Ask your burning questions now, but know that there will be more (and more) questions that arise. This is an ongoing discussion and process of realization and **illumination.**

There is no point seeking a confession
if you do not turn it into a complete ILLUMINATION.

The following 6 questions may be helpful TO ASK as a starting point on the road to full disclosure and true illumination:

These six questions will give you a jump start to begin the deeper discussions needed between you and your partner. Your partner's truthful answers may be painful, but only with truth can you begin to learn about what really happened, address the issues, and heal the vulnerabilities that led to the infidelity in the first place.

- Do you think what you did was wrong? If you think it was wrong, then why did it continue?
- Did you ever stop and consider the effect this would have on me/us/our relationship?
- Did you have feelings for the other person?
- How long has your affair been going on?
- What were they giving you that you couldn't get from me?
- What do you want to do now that I know?

Now you *do* know – you have heard the **confession,** you've asked questions and received answers. You are beginning to fill in the blanks and have the choice to begin to turn the painful truth into an ultimate relationship **ILLUMINATION** and **HEALER** or a relationship destructor.

The outcome of this **ILLUMINATION** is ultimately up to you (and your partner). Yes, it can tear you apart and destroy you if you let it. OR, you can decide that your relationship is worth working on and healing and thus, use this **INFIDELITY** shake up as a wakeup call and opportunity to start afresh.

Either way, you have at least found out the truth, and you have the completion of that part of the story. From now on, it is up to you to heal — either yourself, or yourself and your relationship —in order for you and your partner to either part amicably or deal with this permanently.

You are going to have to face many conflicting and confusing feelings – feelings towards your partner, feelings about yourself and feelings that confront what this betrayal has done to you and the future of your relationship.

"It is better to light a candle than curse the darkness."

Eleanor Roosevelt

CONFRONTATION SUMMARY

- Remain calm, cool, and collected.
- Make sure you have enough proof before confronting infidelity.
- Have a plan in place, and know your purpose.
- DON'T seek out the other guilty party.
- DON'T get caught snooping, but have a story/explanation ready in case you do.
- Never reveal the source of your information.
- Do not make the affair public knowledge.
- Think of this as a mutually beneficial conversation, rather than a confrontation.
- Avoid asking a lot of questions that will put your partner on the defensive.
- Use the OREO COOKIE method.
- Be prepared for defense, deception, distraction, and/or denial.
- Consider seeking the help of a marriage counselor to facilitate communication, defuse emotions, and together confront the whole truth of how and why the cheating occurred.

CHAPTER

6

FOR THE CHEATER

CONFESSING

What to do.
What to avoid.
What to expect.

The allure of **EMOTIONAL SEX** can create the illusion that perfect love truly exists and is right around the corner. Even if your relationship with your 'friend' never develops into anything physical, you're probably already investing a huge amount of attention, appreciation and affection in the other—all of which you should be investing in your primary relationship.

To share this kind of intimacy frequently and regularly with a person outside your primary relationship is at best inappropriate and at worst a lightning rod for destruction.

Think about it—if you are giving all this emotional and sexually flirtatious energy to another, how can you possibly give the **FOOD OF LOVE** to your primary relationship?

Emotional Sex Scenario:

"I have extreme guilt and I don't know how to deal with it. I can't sleep. I keep going over and over in my head how to tell my wife. Or should I tell her? I've asked God for forgiveness but a huge part of me wants my wife's forgiveness too. I really fear how my wife will react to this because I lied to her and she knows and completely despises this woman already. I also know that this would damage the other woman's family too and she could lose her kids if I were to confess. Is it strange that while the affair was going on I was doing everything I could to conceal it, but now that it is definitely over all I can think about is how, when and if I should confess? The damage is already done but I can't seem to move on from my affair with the guilt hanging over me like this!"

Is it better to confess?
Coming clean before you get busted

So, once you realize you're having an affair, the first questions you may ask yourself are, "What if I get caught?" "Should I tell my partner first?"

However, the first question should be -

"Am I ready to end my affair?"

Confessing your affair will certainly aid in bringing your affair to an end. The moment you confess, all hell is going to break loose.

Confessing is helpful if you can't fathom ending your affair on your own, and need your partner's help - in other words, their knowledge of the affair in order for you to pull the plug. It may be the 'drama' needed to shift things into panic mode, so that your action can be swift and decisive.

By not confessing and keeping it a secret, you will reinforce an emotional division between you and your partner that you might never overcome.

If you DO tell your partner **BEFORE** getting busted, there can be life after the storm of confession, where you can rebuild your relationship with your partner - and get a fresh start. This kind of honesty may start a pattern and a process of radical honesty, which is what your primary relationship needs to overcome the secrecy and betrayal of an affair.

Added to this, the chances of you having another affair will probably be slim, precisely because you are taking ownership of your actions and are making the choice to come clean – freely. In addition, it helps establish your credibility when you assert it won't happen again.

So, yes, if you are willing to end your affair and want to tell your partner about it, then do so! But take care to confess with compassionate honesty, understanding, love, and with awareness that YOU are ending the affair.

For good.

5 REASONS YOU SHOULD CONFESS YOUR AFFAIR:

1. Because "What they don't know won't hurt them" is a lie.

Having an open and honest relationship demands that you are transparent and truthful with your partner as well as yourself. Stop kidding yourself that your partner is better off not knowing (because that is convenient for you) and start telling the truth - you know it's the right thing to do.

2. Because the likelihood is your partner already knows.

Whether they find out today or tomorrow or in a decade, they will find out and you will have to deal with this. Deep down they know something is not right and the deception on your part is only adding to their hurt and confusion. Ultimately it will be discovered and made even worse because you kept it hidden despite their suspicions and questions.

3. Because confessing helps heal you AND your relationship.

After the initial shock, there will be punishment from your partner where they remind you again and again of what you have done and how much it hurt. They may initially want to leave or ask you to leave but once the dust settles, and the truthful, heart-centered communication begins, the intimacy will grow and the closeness will deepen. Confessing opens the door to truth. Once your partner understands that you told the truth for the good of your relationship, they will realize that you chose them over the affair and that you really do want to fix what you did wrong.

4. Because not telling about the affair only makes it easier to cheat again.

Do not live in denial - choose truth, it's an infinitely better place to live. Once you see the pain and anguish you have caused, once you have lived with the consequences of your actions, once you see what you have done to those you love, then you will not cheat again.

5. **Because it will facilitate an honest discussion about the state of your relationship—and facilitate improvement and healing.**

By confessing to this affair, you will cause your relationship to go through a crisis, and by going through this crisis you will both be forced to reinvent your relationship together which will ultimately make your relationship stronger and more valuable than ever.

3 REASONS NOT TO CONFESS YOUR AFFAIR:

1. **Because doing so would pose a safety risk.**

If you have cause to believe that confessing the affair would incite your partner to cause harm to yourself or your children or your 'friend', then you should not confess - this is for the greater good. If this is the case, destroy all evidence of the affair and end it immediately.

2. **Because you are ending the relationship with your partner.**

If you do not intend to stay with your partner, then get out now and make it clean. Confessing to the affair would simply cause pain and would serve no productive purpose.

3. **Because your partner couldn't handle the storm.**

If your partner has serious health issues, or has just lost their job, or is under catastrophic stress, a confession at this time may not be wise. It would only add more pain, anxiety and distress to an already full plate.

5 THINGS YOU NEED TO KNOW BEFORE YOU CONFESS:

Plan and prepare what you want to say. This is not the time to be spontaneous and impulsive. It's a weighty topic that deserves care and personal reflection.

However, don't get bogged down aiming for perfection either.

1. Before confessing to your partner, first confess the whole truth and nothing but the truth to YOURSELF.

Taking full responsibility for what you have done is the only way to truly acknowledge that you have been **CHEATING,** which means you have been denying your partner the love, attention and affection they deserve. It is important that you look at the consequences of your actions and inaction.

2. Imagine what all this would feel like in reverse, if your partner had done this to you.

What would you want to have said and done? How would you want to be told? Think about this and then enact it.

3. Understand that your partner's sense of self-esteem, trust, and emotional safety may take a big hit for awhile.

Realize there may be trust issues for a long time, even a lifetime. Be prepared for this reaction and be prepared to put in the time and effort to rebuild that trust. Make it clear that you will do anything to heal the damage that you have caused.

4. Forgive your partner for anything they did (or didn't do) that may have influenced your choice to have EMOTIONAL SEX.

Often, we try to blame our partner or the relationship for our cheating. Do not blame your partner for your affair in any way, now or ever. This will simply add fuel to the fire of breaking up, not making up. They weren't perfect - no one ever is. You both contributed to the holes in the relationship that led to the affair. But, right now, you're the bad one. You're going for productive honesty here; there's no place for anything distracting, blaming or unkind.

5. Watch your body language.

You want to come across as loving, warm, and open, both verbally and non-verbally. Don't cross your arms, which blocks your heart and signals to your partner that you're closing them off. Don't fidget or roll your eyes. Instead, try to do as many of these as possible: leaning in, making eye contact, having a receptive expression, nodding in agreement, breathing in a relaxed manner, and holding your spouse's hand.

THE BEST WAY TO CONFESS TO AN AFFAIR

How to break the news without breaking your partner's heart

Even though you've decided to tell - and it's the brave, right thing to do - the "I confess" part is tough.

It may be one of the hardest things you'll ever have to do.

Let's start with some things you need to know.

> **First**, expect a really **strong reaction**: shock, anger, disbelief, screaming, crying, objects flying through the air, or absolute silence, quiet despair, hurt piercing eyes or cold stare - none of it will be good.

> **Second**, you'll likely be pelted with **questions**: *"How long has this been going on? Are you sleeping with him/her? Are you in LOVE with him/her? How could you do this? Why? Why? Why?"*
>
> Then there may be **accusations**: *"You've been living a double life! You've never loved me!"*

> **Third**, remember no matter how guilty or bad you may be feeling about your **CHEATING**, it is nothing compared to the two-ton truck that is about to shatter your partner's world. While during the affair you may have felt supported, validated and even loved, your partner (consciously or unconsciously) has been feeling your distance, absence and lack of love.

Make sure when you tell your partner about the affair and respond to what they say and ask, that it comes from a place of love and understanding - because your partner is entitled to both.

THE CONFESSION - Using the Oreo Cookie Method
POSITIVE (Love) → NEGATIVE (the tough stuff) → POSITIVE (Love)

START your confession **with love**, by opening with something such as, *"I love you. I am telling you this because I want for us to have a strong, loving, honest relationship. I really screwed up. I feel the only way we can move forward and build a strong relationship is by being totally honest. I want to tell you the truth so that we can move on and heal our relationship together."*

Then, tell what happened - how and why it began (but without too many details).

At this moment, your partner doesn't need to know a lot - only that you've been leaning on someone else and having misplaced emotions; that you've realized this was energy and focus that should have been given solely to them. Trust me, the questions and the requests for vivid explanations (which you'd be wise to avoid right now) will be coming soon.

Then, **close with love**. *"I love you. I want to focus on making our relationship work. I am so sorry that I hurt and betrayed you. I will do anything to make it right between us again."*

Be empathetic even before your partner knows that they need your empathy. Understand and take responsibility for what you know is wrong, and close with love.

IF YOU DO GET CAUGHT AND CONFRONTED

When you're suddenly accused of wrongdoing - or even caught clearly in the act - it's human instinct to want to PROTECT yourself.

But if you want to SAVE your relationship...

⊗ DON'T:

⊗ Deny

⊗ Defend (offering excuses and explanations)

⊗ Distract

⊗ Withdraw

⊗ Blame and attack back

⊗ Apologize prematurely or insincerely to escape punishment or disfavor

These are all actions of FEAR.

- FEAR is the opposite of love -

While these tactics are self-protective in nature, they are relationship destructors. They perpetuate more emotional separation, distrust and communication breakdown.

Besides, your partner probably already KNOWS a lot - that's why you are being confronted.

Your partner most likely has proof

They may have been suspicious for a while, building their case.

- Find out what they do know.
- Avoid getting defensive.
- Lean in, not away.
- You may want to deflect by turning it around and blaming – don't.
- Your partner may be emotional, accusatory, upset – STAY CALM

Don't offer an immediate excuse or explanation, and don't say *"I'm sorry, BUT...."* The *"but"* signals a major cop-out on your part because it's a way of blaming your partner and dodging responsibility for your actions.

Explanations generally work best after you have acknowledged your partner's feelings and have given a sincere apology. The best time to give an explanation is when your partner asks for one. If you blurt out an explanation too quickly, it can seem like an excuse or way of getting out of trouble; in other words, babbling undermines credibility.

When explaining, be constructive, not blaming. Focus on your feelings underlying what happened, not your partner's behavior. For example, emphasize *"I felt lonely and invisible, even when you were around"* as opposed to saying, *"You always work late hours and when you do come home, you flat out ignore me."* This is the time to be sincere, but also remorseful, sensitive and sympathetic of your partner's pain.

Don't apologize too quickly, it can sound insincere. You may want to try to appease your partner or protect yourself by rushing to an apology, hoping that this will calm your partner and get them to back off. Your words and heart need to be thoughtful, meaningful, and sincere. First, hear your partner out. Wait to apologize until you and your partner can discuss the situation.

Don't be a drama queen/king by blaming yourself in an exaggerated way. By staging a pity party, you're only trying to disarm your partner from criticizing you, by beating him/her to the punch. It's dishonest and counter-productive .

Watch your body language. If you're giving an explanation through clenched teeth, it's insulting and not believable and will only increase the tension in an already difficult situation.

HOW TO SAY "I'M SORRY" AND GIVE A GOOD APOLOGY

Many people have a hard time admitting they've done something wrong or hurtful, and then apologizing for it.

Apologize not just for the affair but for the harm you have done to your partner's feelings and to the stability of the relationship between the two of you. Saying, *"I am sorry"* with total sincerity can lead to a better chance of forgiveness, honest communication, repair of trust, and hopefully less punishment or retribution later.

• **Think of the 4 R's**

RECOGNIZE *and acknowledge the pain you have caused.*

Express **REGRET/REMORSE** *about what you've done and the pain it caused.*

Take **RESPONSIBILITY** *for your actions.*

Express your desire to **RECONCILE/REMEDY/MAKE RESTITUTION** *to give your partner what they need to feel safe.*

For an apology to be effective, it must be clear that you accept full responsibility for your actions and inactions. After all, you didn't mess up because of your partner, you did it through your own actions and poor choices. You must also be willing to abide by your partner's request for remedying the situation, such as staying off Facebook or ceasing all contact with your affair partner. Agree to do whatever it takes for your partner to feel safe and rebuild trust, and then follow through.

ASKING FOR FORGIVENESS

Confession and an apology are the first steps of stopping the damage and starting the repair phase of your relationship.

But there is a critical next step: asking for and receiving forgiveness from your partner.

Seeking forgiveness after being unfaithful is truly the first step of the healing process. It is a step that cannot be skipped but may take the longest to receive.

You may not receive forgiveness right away, or it may come in stages.

You will probably have to say *"I am sorry, I want to rebuild our relationship"* over and over again and allow your life to be an open book to your partner.

You may feel you are being supervised and treated like a child every time you log onto the computer or leave the house, but you need to abide by whatever remedies and restitution (remember those 4 R's?) the two of you agreed to. (I will go into more detail in the Trust section of this book).

Always keep in mind that if you had to forgive your partner, it would be hard when you feel so hurt, wouldn't it? So allow the healing process to take whatever time is necessary.

Will your partner forgive you —
either now or in the future?
There are no guarantees

➡ Innocent partners react differently to the news and it is hard to predict.

➡ Some may be closed-minded and think, "The trust is gone, and so am I."

➡ With others, it might be, "Huh. Just the ticket I need - I wanted out before, and here's my chance to escape without looking like the bad guy."

➡ But often people pull back emotionally for a time, isolate themselves and digest what they've been told.

* **If your partner loves you and they want things to work out, they will gradually see that your confession is about the renewal of truth and changing the elements of your relationship that led to the affair.**

If you can hold your ground, maintain your honesty and face the storm head on, then you will show your partner that you want this relationship to work as well...

And slowly, ever so slowly the trust will be regained and the love will be restored.

CHAPTER

7

FOR THE CHEATER

ENDING YOUR AFFAIR

HAVE YOU ENDED THE AFFAIR?

If not, are you really ready?

Do you want your primary relationship to be renewed or end? Because something's got to give. You cannot continue to split yourself between two worlds. The energy and time you are giving to one relationship IS being taken from the other, plain and simple.

Whatever this affair is—even if it's *just* emotional—the truth is this: it DOES hurt your primary relationship. In fact, **EMOTIONAL SEX** is more damaging than physical intimacy alone. Your affair is weakening the bonds of your primary relationship, even if your partner DOES NOT KNOW about it because *when you are emotionally involved and intoxicated with another person, you are unable to give your full attention and love to your primary relationship.* You simply cannot nurture (or repair) your primary partnership if you are NOT fully present physically, mentally or emotionally with your partner (or yourself). At this point, you're simply committed in name, but not in spirit.

If you want to make your primary relationship work, you're going to have to *really* end the affair - and for the right reasons - otherwise you may be too tempted to run back to it.

Are you really ready to end your affair for the right reasons?

- ✅ You want to end the affair because your primary partner is the most important person to you.
- ✅ You want to make your REAL relationship work and not end.
- ✅ After much thought and deliberation, you are clear as to why the affair started in the first place - and also why it must end.
- ✅ You are prepared to let go of your lover.
- ✅ You're tired of the lies and cover-ups.
- ✅ You have a self-care plan in place.

If you answered YES to these, it sounds like you are ready to make the break.

However...

Here are a few more questions I suggest you ask yourself:

- ❓ Is your only motivation the fear of getting caught?
- ❓ Are you being forced to do this because you've been busted?
- ❓ Is the choice to end the affair and return to your partner financially motivated?
- ❓ Do you believe that only your 'friend' understands and values the real you?

If you said YES to any of these latest questions, you may not be truly committed to breaking away from your friend and making the break permanent - you may need to seek counseling to delve further into your reasons for having the affair and why you're having such difficulty leaving it behind.

AFTER EMOTIONAL SEX CAN THIS RELATIONSHIP GO BACK TO BEING A PLATONIC FRIENDSHIP?

This is rare but it can be done. *(see * caveat below)*

There are **three** steps that can transition this affair away from deception:

1. You and your friend have to openly agree that platonic friendship is what you both want and remain steadfast and clean about it. No wavering, no 'gray' areas.

2. Bring your new friend home and introduce him/her to your partner and family - it's about time that he/she is made a family friend rather than your exclusive pal. (Your real partner needs to be 100% comfortable with this, especially after understanding the truth about the relationship you had with your friend).

3. Come clean with your partner (tell the whole truth) and begin to work on the holes that created room for an affair in the first place.

*However, one important caveat. Ending an affair is hard work as you will soon see. Make sure that you aren't kidding yourself, or worse, continuing the deception with the illusion that you can turn this into a REAL platonic friendship.

Take the affair out of the dark
                              and into the light

CAN A PHYSICAL AFFAIR GO BACK TO PLATONIC FRIENDSHIP?

When it comes to ending your physical affair and becoming platonic friends, the process is especially tricky, takes a very long time and is not recommended. Before considering a friendship with your lover, you must first end the affair completely, entirely and finally. This involves ceasing all communication and contact and truly letting all sparks of attraction, desire, and feelings between you die. This can take years. The illusion of remaining friends is often a cover up for wanting to circumvent or avoid the feelings of loss and withdrawal you are afraid to feel or is a way to keep the door open between you and your lover and not really end the affair. Give it time and give it space. Don't fool yourself.

The essential part of healing with your primary partner after a physical affair is that you address the issues that led to the affair and you work on those issues with your relationship partner honestly, openly, and lovingly. Having the distraction of your lover, hanging around in the background, no matter what you call this lover (i.e. platonic friend) will ONLY complicate and undermine your partnership healing.

HOW TO DEAL WITH THE ENDING OF THE AFFAIR

As we discussed in the earlier section on brain chemistry and love, this isn't just a matter of willpower.

EMOTIONAL SEX is a lot like being addicted to a drug

Biochemical research has shown that the effect of 'love chemicals' is twofold - they are released in RESPONSE to your excitement about your friend, and they BOND you to your friend.

This is especially true for women who produce high levels of oxytocin, the bonding chemical that enhances the feeling of having found your soul mate.

When your brain and body start releasing addicting 'love' chemicals, you feel so good, you don't want your affair to end. It almost feels as if you would **perish without contact**. Your connection feels genuine, romantic, even **life-sustaining**. Letting go of such intoxicating 'nourishment' seems unimaginable, when you're feeling so safe, so right, so fulfilled by it.

Or so it would appear.

Emotional Sex Scenario:

"When my husband came across my romantic emails to Curtis, I came clean, showed him all the emails and promised to end the interactions immediately. But I couldn't. I couldn't stop, I couldn't help myself. The more I tried to forget Curtis, the more I was consumed by him. I kept checking his Facebook page to see if his relationship status had changed, if he had met someone new, if there were any signs he had moved on and forgotten me. I couldn't even defriend him or remove his number from my cell phone. I was overwhelmed with guilt, knowing how much time I was spending on this instead of with my family, but I just wasn't ready to call it quits."

COMING 'CLEAN' AND MOVING AWAY FROM THE OTHER PERSON

Once you've made the decision and the commitment to end the affair and rebuild your primary relationship, it's important to understand what you may be going through emotionally, physically, and psychologically during this process.

It is not as easy as saying, *"Okay, it's over"* – feelings linger and can become obsessive or guilt-ridden, and situations can be particularly touchy if the affair was with a co-worker, neighbor, or partner of a friend.

Let's look at the reality and the solutions for these issues and more.

If We Didn't Have Physical Sex, Will the Break-up Be a Breeze?

So you're saying to yourself, this will be pretty easy, because we never had sex.

The opposite might be true.

EMOTIONAL SEX can turn particularly obsessive especially because there was never sex to consummate the romantic fantasies.

There can be the sense of 'unfinished business' or the ongoing fantasy that the sex and relationship would have been great if you were together.

It feels like you are severing your connection with your Best Friend.

HOW TO END YOUR AFFAIR WITH CLASS AND CLARITY

✅ **Break off all involvement immediately.**

I wholeheartedly agree with other experts who recommend that you go cold turkey - you're giving up an addiction, remember?

End it, by flushing your proverbial 'stash' down the toilet - delete all text messages, emails, throw away any gifts or other reminders of your time together, and then erase all contact info you have stored everywhere.

'De-friend' in every way.

✅ **MAKE IT CLEAR – to yourself and your affair partner – THAT IT'S FINAL.**

Once it's FINAL there is no 'occasional interaction'. NO check ins and chats. NO long, never-ending goodbyes. NO after work get-togethers even in a group setting. NO texting, emailing or calling. NO 'we're just friends now'. If this is a work colleague, keep things strictly professional. You can do it! Just keep reminding yourself you've got a fresh new start, and things are changing for the better - expect and prepare for withdrawal.

Cold as it seems, don't do the breakup in person - there is too much temptation to waiver, as you are both too vulnerable.

Send an email or text asking to arrange a time to speak by phone. Explain that you realize your *'friendship'* is posing a threat to your primary relationship and that you respectfully request that the two of you have no further contact. Be firm in stating that this is what's best for you and your primary relationship, and that you wish the person well.

Be clear, but be kind.

Your friend may feel shocked, devastated and rejected. You can be compassionate and considerate, but do not back pedal! Give no mixed messages. Say goodbye and that you can't see or talk to them ever again. Don't say *"I will always love you"* or *"Maybe we can connect when everything settles down in my life."* No! You've got to close the open emotional door and cut off all contact. Period.

It's a little more complicated if you work with your friend.

You obviously need to end things without risking your job or reputation with colleagues. So don't break up at work. Ask your affair partner to respect your privacy and interact ONLY for work-related purposes. Creating new emotional boundaries is tricky. Do everything possible to move your office or cubicle so that you don't see your friend. Keep all discussions strictly business related. Stop all personal texts, calls, and conversations. Do not stop by their office or desk to chat. You may need to transfer to another department or facility. If the situation remains uncomfortable and affects your job performance, you may need to find a new job.

If your affair is a cyber affair that has either remained online or has led to phone calls and/or in-person contact, you must greatly reduce your time online.

You have to break your addiction to the person and the website or chat room involved. Use your computer only for business, family, and non-affair personal reasons. If your partner asks you to stop using the computer entirely, to help rebuild trust, do so if at all practical. Stop visiting any social media sites, chat rooms, forum, or interest groups where you met your friend and where you have had contact with him or her. Defriend that person on Facebook. Block them if they try to contact you. You'll be amazed at how much time you suddenly have to spend with your family.

DO NOT ATTEMPT TO CONTACT YOUR 'FRIEND' FOR ANY REASON.

YOU'VE ENDED IT -

Be Prepared for Withdrawal Symptoms

(Remember, Your Brain is Truly Addicted to Love)

Your best friends, your partner, and your inner critic will probably just tell you *"Get over it. Move on. You were just hurting yourself and everyone around you."* Easy to say. Much harder to do.

The end of an emotional or physical affair causes your brain and body to go through **actual withdrawal symptoms**.

You have to face the fact that there is addiction with love, and the fantasy and emotional connection that comes with **EMOTIONAL SEX**.

Your brain has been trained to use LOVE
        as a fast way to feel good and get a
                chemical high

This means that when you end the affair you will have to go through the uncomfortable experience of withdrawal before you can be 'clean' again.

You're going to need to be both tough and nurturing with yourself to get through this.

Let's start with what might happen, so you can be prepared, and even discuss this with your partner in advance so you are both prepared.

Be realistic, your partner may be in no mood to empathize with you, and may even feel you deserve this 'punishment' for what you did to the relationship. It is unlikely that you will be getting a great deal of positive feedback from your partner at this point and this is bound to make you feel emotionally disconnected – which can worsen your withdrawal symptoms.

Let's revisit **Phenethylamine** (PEA). This is the chemical that gives you that thrill and upsurge in energy when you fall in love. So what happens when you drop that person from your life? Your PEA levels drop, too. This can lead to psychological reactions that cause obsessive preoccupation with your affair partner and an overwhelming desire to pull that person back into your life. Then, when you feel you can't stop desiring or needing that person, you may experience the added feelings of guilt, shame or hopelessness. Just know that the mood swings and emotions are real and chemically based. Take consolation in the fact that you're battling actual withdrawal and resolve to win!

You've experienced a loss, a death of sorts, an important person will no longer be in your life. It doesn't matter if it was a cyber affair, strictly emotional, or was physical. You will feel a vacuum - a void.

• • • •

When you're dreaming with a broken heart
The waking up is the hardest part
You roll outta bed and down on your knees
And for the moment you can hardly breathe
Wondering was she really here?
Is she standing in my room?
No she's not, 'cause she's gone, gone, gone, gone, gone....

Dreaming With A Broken Heart by JOHN MAYER

 Your reaction can include:

- Grief
- Despair
- Sadness
- Loneliness
- Obsessive thinking
- Feeling like you're falling apart or that your heart is breaking

How Can I Handle These Feelings and Recover?

In order to move on, heal your relationship, and recover, you have to first heal yourself. If you feel that you have had your needs met in this affair in a way that hasn't been met in your relationship, there is going to be a time when you need to address those problems with your partner. However, it's too soon and raw right after a confession, apology, and attempt at reconciliation. Allow some time for things to calm down and normalize between the two of you. Cooler heads will allow you both to speak and be heard in a way that is supportive and will help your relationship grow.

This is a time to take a hard look at any needs and emotions that are being unmet within yourself that made **you** vulnerable to **EMOTIONAL SEX.** When you have more interests in your life and feel more fulfilled, you will be less vulnerable or needy of finding something or someone exciting or taboo to entice you. It's vital to nurture yourself while you are simultaneously trying to heal your relationship and let go of your lover. In general, I recommend that you take care of yourself in four core areas: **physically, emotionally, mentally** and **spiritually,** in ways that resonate with you in each of these areas.

Here are a few suggestions to get you started on a self-care, fulfillment plan.

- ✓ **Funnel the energy, time and attention** you were putting into your affair back into your primary relationship. Spend more time with your partner with the goal of getting closer and having fun together. Communicate, rediscover, find new, interesting ways to talk, learn, and connect in a healthier, more complete way.

- ✓ **Focus on gratitude.** Gratitude is the 'get of jail' card for your heart. It can transform pain into love, confusion into clarity, and bring peace to your emotional chaos. So quiet down, take 3 deep breaths, and remind yourself of all the things BIG and SMALL that you are thankful for.

- ✓ **Get up and out of the house**, and back in the land of the living. This is especially true if you are feeling depressed because your first instinct could be to stay in bed with the curtains closed, which won't do a whole lot for your self-image OR your partner's attraction to you!

- ✓ **Exercise!** It increases your dopamine levels.

- ✓ **Get some sun**—the bright and uplifting light will improve your mood!

- ✓ **Avoid sliding into destructive behavior** such as isolating yourself from others and eating and drinking too much. Sure, eating chocolate will boost some neurotransmitters for a while, but too much alcohol and gorging on sweets and fatty foods only stuffs down your feelings, which can cause you to be unhealthy and start feeling even worse about yourself. Get enough sleep. Consciously breathe deep, calming breaths. Take breaks several times a day. This is a great time to eat healthy and give yourself the nutrients for the physical and psychological stamina you will need. Plus, caring and nurturing yourself does wonders for your well-being!

- ✓ **Watch something funny** on TV or hit a comedy club. Or, just laugh with friends - it is the best medicine. Also, when you get together with happy people, your face mirrors their happy expressions and can trigger a happy reaction throughout your body.

✅ **Face the fact that you got yourself into this mess,** so face the feelings, too. Try journaling to help face the mix of emotions, and set them free.

✅ **Use your senses** to reinforce positive messages to yourself through visualization, positive self-talk, affirmations or prayer.

✅ **Do anything constructive** that shows you are treating yourself with tenderness: take good care of yourself. This will help counter the self-criticism as well as any judging behavior from your partner.

✅ **Connect with your partner** as much as you can, and keep working on rebuilding the relationship. Action forward helps the situation move away from the past.

✅ **Talk to friends,** a therapist or spiritual leader at your place of worship.

✅ **Turn the guilt into something positive.** It can be a great motivator to become even more involved with your partner and family. Let your partner know how bad you feel and how much you wish to make amends. Find out what they need and what you can do to change the situation for the better. Life is about second chances—so try to stop beating yourself up.

Let yourself go through the stages of grief. Don't just stuff your feelings down — denial only postpones facing the feelings and situation, as well as recovery.

I'M OBSESSING ABOUT MY LOVER. MAKE IT STOP!

Emotional Sex Scenario:

"Ouch! I'm hurting bad. I know that ending it is what I had to do, my heart isn't agreeing with my brain. It feels unbearable to not be able to talk with him every day like I used to. I'm trying to appreciate my husband and the family I have, but all I can think about is how much I miss him and would love to talk to him."

Take peace from knowing that it is normal and logical to obsess about your now ex-lover. I'm not trying to downplay the effect, mind you, but to let you know that your obsession actually makes sense. You two were totally focused on each other - sharing communication, love, nurturing attention and support. At a minimum, this person provided a distraction and escape from the mundane routine or stressful overwhelm of your life. Now there's a huge emotional void. The withdrawal symptoms are so uncomfortable, it's natural to crave, desire and obsess about the person. But you must NOT indulge your craving. If you reconnect you will only risk becoming reattached and undoing all the healthy progress that you have made.

How to make the obsession stop

When you indulge in obsessing, it keeps the addiction and connection to your 'lover' strong. You've got to funnel the energy you were giving to your 'lover' back to your primary relationship, your partner, and yourself. Now is the time to re-channel this energy back *home*.

Try these proven tips:

⊃ **Schedule some obsessing time.** If an obsessive thought enters your mind, tell it that you have scheduled it for a specific time each day or night. Then, when your scheduled obsessing time arrives, go ahead and obsess for the appointed period (a few minutes), or postpone it to another. Never exceed those few minutes - set a timer, if necessary, and have the DING! command an end to your session. Hopefully, you will choose to postpone more frequently until the obsessive thoughts fade away.

⊃ **When you find yourself obsessing** at other times, literally tell yourself to STOP! Say it in your mind to yourself. Say it out loud, if you can. Visualize a big red stop sign in your mind. Say it over and over if you need to: "Stop! Stop! STOP!"

⊃ **Instead of remembering the pleasure,** focus on what a mess you got yourself into and how much pain this created for your family.

⊃ **If you can't stop idealizing your lover,** try imagining or writing down some 'reality checks' - something really humanizing, such as what it would be like to share a bathroom with this person. Focus on some of his/her qualities that weren't so endearing - I guarantee you noticed some! Stick a pin in that fantasy bubble and listen to it 'pop.'

⊃ **Get rid of anything** that could trigger memories of your affair. That means removing or throwing out love letters, emails, photos, souvenirs and gifts. Come on! There is NO good reason to keep them. And you know it.

WHAT IF I WANT TO CALL, WRITE OR CONNECT WITH MY LOVER?

*You've got to LEARN faithfulness in order
to not cheat again.
Don't expect it to come **naturally***

Begin by making a personal pact to walk an unwavering line of honesty.

Assert to yourself that you are a person of uncompromising integrity. And, if (or rather when) you feel yourself start to stray like a weak moth drawn to the flame of infidelity, or sense yourself rationalizing any kind of cheating behavior, strongly tell yourself 'NO!' and willfully reject the opportunity.

You have a new bond now with yourself and your partner that you will not break at any cost.

Repeat after me....
Sacrificing what I've just begun to rebuild is
NOT an option

NO MATTER HOW BAD YOU FEEL ABOUT ENDING YOUR AFFAIR, YOUR PARTNER IS FEELING WORSE

No matter how much personal hell you may put yourself through, no matter how horrible the emotional or physical toll, your spouse will be suffering more - far more.

While you've been consumed by euphoria - the intoxicating, mutual love and desire for someone and something new - your partner is suddenly slammed with the knowledge that you've been cheating and the reality that the relationship they thought you had together has been instantaneously redefined.

Imagine your partner's shock of going from feeling loved and secure to feeling rejected, unloved, diminished, unsure, vulnerable, and utterly alone—all in a nanosecond as the horrible secret is revealed.

The betrayed suffers more than the betrayer.

CHAPTER

8

FOR THE BETRAYED

Healing Through the Trauma, Stress, Grief and Betrayal

of Cyber, Emotional, and/or Physical Affairs

Emotional Sex Scenario:

"I just found out my girlfriend of 3 years has been having an affair with her ex for the past 6 months. I feel completely gutted, and like my very world has been turned on its head. She says she loves us both, but wants to be with me. I'm totally devastated."

Betrayal is a broken agreement -
I trusted you and you deceived me

Betrayal smashes your world to the very core, throwing you into the depths of despair. Added to this, you can feel totally alone and isolated since the one person in the world you were building a life with has completely trashed your feelings and emotions.

Your precise reactions - your thoughts and feelings - will depend somewhat on whether your discovery of the infidelity was a total shock or you had been suspicious for some time.

The trust you might have once shared is now on

life support

The fact that you were betrayed, the fact that you let this go unnoticed for however long it was may lead to you doubting yourself.

You will also be doubting the integrity of your partner (as you should) and the future of your relationship together.

"Betrayal is the only truth that sticks."

Arthur Miller

Betrayal is tied into abandonment and loss.

You may want to hurt your spouse, get even, or walk away.

The physical and mental state you are in might be overwhelming.

Your body shakes and shivers, your heart pounds, your stomach aches.

Did YOU know?
When feelings are strong they tend to drive our actions After some reflection we might regret our behavior

Your mind races with feelings of anger and shock, disappointment and hurt, confusion and despair, shame and disbelief.

Did YOU know?
In an emotional crisis our attention locks in on the problem and we start obsessing

Your self-esteem and your sense of relationship continuity, emotional safety and trust may be completely rattled to the core.

These feelings are real signs
of the pain and hurt within
and do need to be faced rather than suppressed

However,
try not to act on feelings alone.

RIGHT NOW IS A REALLY BAD TIME TO MAKE LIFE-CHANGING DECISIONS

Initially surviving infidelity means nothing more than letting the fog rise.

Give yourself some time to calm down a bit, feel your feelings, get your thoughts straight, and take care of yourself.

Only when you start to feel a little better, can you begin to consider what your next step should be.

Did
YOU know?

When you are STRESSED
Your emotional brain
(or limbic system)   sends
cortisol raging through
your body,
making it difficult to
think straight

Emotional Sex Scenario:

"I recently found out that my wife has been having an affair for the past nine months. When I confronted her, she denied it at first, then confessed once I showed her the emails I had found on her computer and the calls and texts to 'him' on her cell phone. She says that it's over, and she only loves me and wants to be with me. I can't articulate what I'm feeling. It hurts so much! I feel betrayed beyond measure. To think that after eight years of an incredible marriage, the woman that I love more than anything could do something like this to me - to us. It's like stabbing me in the heart, over and over again.

I have been nothing but a faithful husband and a good father to our kids. I loved and supported her through all the various ups and downs our relationship has gone through. I helped her out with the kids whenever I could, I dedicated my entire weekends to her and the family. What more could I do? I thought I was giving her everything, my entire self, physically and emotionally, but I guess there's something that I wasn't providing. What is it? She continues to apologize, profess her love, and ask for my forgiveness. We've both cried, are becoming close again, and are communicating better than before. I want to forgive her because of how we feel towards each other. But I feel that she's still hiding some secrets from me and she's not telling me the whole truth. I also keep asking myself, "Is she really over this guy? Would she, could she ever do anything like this again?" If we are to get past this, how can I ever fully trust her again? Deep down, I'm drowning in so much pain, it's hard to function. I can't sleep. I can't eat. I keep saying...'How could she have done this to me?'

Knowing What to Expect Makes the Passage Easier

Life is always easier to handle when we have some idea of what we may be subjected to at any given moment.

Once you have experienced a deep betrayal such as this, it is not unusual to:

- ➲ Cry at the drop of a hat.
- ➲ Experience a deep sense of loss.
- ➲ Feel irritated and angry with 'trivia.'
- ➲ Feel like everything is too much of an effort.
- ➲ Evade people who you do not want to inform.
- ➲ Not have the energy to consider how to get over the affair.
- ➲ Have difficulty thinking, concentrating and retaining information.
- ➲ Be consumed by a sense of hurt and anger and even vengefulness.
- ➲ Feel tired all the time and have sleep problems (too little or too much).
- ➲ Experience physical reactions such as nausea, diarrhea, shakiness, binge eating and not wanting to eat.
- ➲ Feel overwhelmed with strong emotions - uncertainty, fear, rejection, shame, loss of hope, disappointment, agitation, irritation, anger, frustration, sadness, despair, amongst others.

I have never met anyone who hasn't experienced these emotions (in some blend) after the discovery of an affair - the journey to healing is often like a roller coaster ride.

At times you may feel like you're progressing quite well, only to be activated by a reminder and whoosh, the pain is back as if it just happened.

Do not be disheartened. It doesn't mean you aren't healing. It means you are normal.

LET YOURSELF GRIEVE

 The Grieving Process

Going through the process of grief over the loss of trust and the sense of being betrayed is akin to mourning and grieving the death of a loved one.

Victims of infidelity often report emotions and feelings similar to those of widows or widowers:

- They feel abandoned.
- They feel alone in their grief.
- They feel terrified of the future.
- They feel disconnected from other couples and friends.
- They feel as if they could have done something to prevent this.
- They have a lot of unfinished business with their spouse that is now off-limits or has been overshadowed by what has occurred.
- They feel they should be doing better than they are for the time that they've been going through the pain.
- They will even pretend nothing has happened (such as the widow who sets a plate for the lost partner at the dinner table).

Grieving is not only natural, it is important. Processing that grief feels complicated and excruciating. Organizing your thoughts about the grief you feel is essential in order for you to overcome the painful emotions and get through this in the best way possible.

The physical pain, anxiety attacks, and the roller coaster of depression and feeling shattered into millions of pieces does not mean you're going crazy.

Your Body, Brain and Emotional Systems
are going through MAJOR STRESS

STRESS is the body's way of protecting you and keeping you on your toes in times of danger.

If the stress response is constantly activated, the body is basically on red alert and will soon be worn down.

When your relationship is threatened, your body's defense system will kick in automatically. This defense system manifests itself as a 'stress response' that is sometimes known as 'fight or flight.' The response of your nervous system releases a flood of stress hormones that rouse your body for emergency action.

These physical changes cause your heart to pound faster, your muscles to tighten, your blood pressure to rise, your breath to quicken, and your senses to become sharper. Your strength and stamina are heightened, your speed and reaction time are increased, and your focus is enhanced, preparing you to either fight or fly from the danger at hand.

The stress response
is the body's way of protecting you

The stress response system is designed to save your life in an emergency so that you have the strength to get out of danger or the speed to avoid it.

When working properly, it helps you stay focused, energetic, and alert.

But relentless stress causes major damage to your life; affecting your health, mood, productivity, and relationships.

Did
YOU know?

Your MIND and
the BODY are
linked

The long-term activation of the stress-response system and the subsequent overexposure to cortisol and other stress hormones can disrupt almost all your body's processes.

Higher and more prolonged levels of cortisol in the bloodstream can negatively affect your immune system and decrease the number of brain cells, thereby impairing your memory and putting you at increased risk of numerous health problems.

Normally, after an episode of danger, the brain returns itself to normal and banishes the cortisol to the kidneys where it can exit the body.

However, if the perceived threat does not pass (e.g. thinking about the affair, obsessing about the affair, over-focusing on the affair), cortisol remains in the brain, stressing you out to the max.

The activities you engage in and the daily choices you make affect the way you feel physically and emotionally.

When you take care of your body, learn how to stay calm, be good to yourself, get enough rest and eat healthy foods, you'll automatically experience greater mental and emotional well-being.

For example, exercise is a powerful antidote to stress, not only because it strengthens your heart and lungs, but it also releases endorphins, powerful chemicals that energize you and lift your mood.

Regaining balance and banishing cortisol after an episode of stress is not difficult and gets easier with practice.

If you do not manage your STRESS levels
even day-to-day living can contribute
to your body's stress response

STRESS causes physical damage to your body.

STRESS and obsessive thinking are a threat to your health.

STRESS can be *turned off* if you acknowledge its presence and **consciously take time to relax** so that the normal, healthy chemicals will return to dominance in your brain.

Relaxing *is a learned skill*
that you can practice very easily

It's easy because you already know *how to do it.*

Mindful deep breathing is a simple and powerful way to get your STRESS levels in check.

Mindful deep breathing automatically reduces your STRESS hormones, slows down your heart rate, lowers your blood pressure and relaxes your muscles.

Relaxation increases energy and focus, relieves aches and pains, heightens problem-solving abilities, combats illness, boosts motivation and productivity.

Did YOU know? **Relaxation is literally *a breath away...***

TRY IT NOW!
RIGHT WHERE YOU ARE

... as you read this, breathe deeply, carefully, powerfully...

Instant Stress Antidote —
Practice Deep Breathing

The key to deep breathing is to breathe deeply from your abdomen, getting as much fresh air as possible into your lungs.

When you take slow deep breaths, the oxygen you take in will help you relax.

Anytime you feel stressed, take a minute, slow down and breathe deeply:

- Sit comfortably.
- Breathe in through your nose... to the count of 3.
- Exhale through your mouth... to the count of 3.
- Continue to breathe in through your nose 1-2-3 and out through your mouth 1-2-3.

The next time you feel the stress rising, the anxiety attacking, or the obsessive thinking taking over, be it... in your car, in the shower, at your desk, on the computer, talking to your partner, while watching TV...

Take a pause. Tune IN. And, take a deep, slow BREATH. And then, another.

The more you *breathe deeply* and *meaningfully*
the more able you will be to overcome the STRESS
and *cope* with the **trauma** you are experiencing

Emotional Sex Scenario:

"It's been two weeks since my wife told (confessed to) me about the affair she had. She has ended it and cut off all avenues of communication. The guy's parting comments in a text, no less, were that he knows that he's "the one" and "will wait for her as long as it takes." I had no idea that I was capable of feeling such murderous rage! I feel like I have been emotionally gutted like a fish. Talk about a roller coaster ride. We've had one session of marital counseling and I feel some hope, along with a host of other not so pretty emotions... My wife and I have been through a lot in 18 years of marriage, but this is by far the most hurtful thing I have ever experienced."

HOW TO COPE WITH THE AFTERMATH:

GIVE YOURSELF THE OXYGEN FIRST.

As they tell you on airplanes,
PUT THE MASK ON YOUR OWN FACE FIRST;
THEN ON YOUR RELATIONSHIP

If someone you loved was traumatized, how would you take care of them? How would you hold them? What would you be telling them?

This is the time to take the energy you've invested into your now traumatized relationship and put some of that energy back into nurturing yourself.

TAKE CARE OF YOURSELF

Rebuild yourself from the ground up.

Be very kind and gentle with yourself.

Balance is the key to getting through this experience of betrayal.

"Let's face the moment
rather than turn away from it."

David Deida - Intimate Communion

SELF LOVE CPR

*Care, Protect, Resuscitate your
body, mind and spirit*

Take care of your body. Feel your feelings.
Control your thinking.

**Take Care of Your BODY**

Physical Signs of Distress:

I can't eat, sleep, or think straight.

Looking after your body
will look after your mind

Here are 5 tips for you to bear in mind:

1. Do not abuse substances or medications.

2. Eat healthily and regularly.

3. Get plenty of sleep.

4. Let yourself laugh.

5. Exercise.

REGAINING YOUR BALANCE

1. ## Meditate Instead of Medicate

Substances (drugs, alcohol, cigarettes, coffee) are devastating to your body and mind. Medications should only ever be taken in accordance with the dosage recommended. In times of stress it may be tempting to over medicate or abuse, but this will only impair your sleep patterns and cause you to spiral downward into depression.

2. ## Mindful Eating

Eating well and drinking water are essential to your body receiving the nutrients it needs to function properly. Treat yourself as if you were your own child — eat good, wholesome meals that are balanced and freshly made.

3. ## Decide to Dream Beautiful Dreams

Sleep is essential for you to function in an optimum fashion — both mentally and physically. If you are having trouble going to sleep, because of *punishing, pain-producing thoughts,* try this. Keep a journal by your bed, write down your anxieties, and imagine them flowing OUT of YOU and onto the paper. Say *"I fully release you and let you go." "I give myself permission to peacefully sleep."*

4. ## Smile... And the World Smiles With You

The simple things can make you smile - time with friends or even a child you enjoy, a movie, a massage, a picnic in the park or a snowball fight. Do whatever you can do to get you out of your zone and put a smile on your face. One smile leads to another, and then, to another.

5. ## Exercise is Excellent

Exercise is the enemy of stress, depression, and anxiety. It is the natural way to calm your body and alleviate the negative emotions that you may be feeling. Do something physical for your body every day: park far away from the entrance to the supermarket, take the stairs instead of the elevator, walk to work. Try to get in 30 minutes a day to raise your temperature and lift your mood.

THE BENEFITS OF MEDITATION

Meditation does not need to be difficult -
it should be mindful, not a chore

The goal of meditation is to *stop the obsessive chatter of the mind.*

It would be great if you could just say, "STOP!" to the emotional bombardment that is assaulting your life - but your mind doesn't work that way. It helps you re-focus if you re-apply your thoughts to something different, something positive.

I find it helps if I do not necessarily 'decide' to meditate, but instead, I decide to take in the value of the world around me - the sounds I hear, the sights I see, the objects I feel, the sensations all around me everyday. Be it the sounds of my footsteps, the view in the park, the softness of a sweater or the crackling of an autumn leaf.

By focusing on the details of the world we are drawn away from the details in our mind.

By slowing down and appreciating the world around us we distract ourselves from the dark side and attract good thoughts.

If we slow down, we are more deliberate...
more deliberate *in our breath, more*
deliberate *in our thoughts*

‣ Breathing deeply and mindfully is meditation.

‣ Breathing deeply loads your brain and body with oxygen.

‣ Breathing deeply allows your body to relax and replenish.

‣ Breathing deeply is the most positive and beneficial exercise you can do for your mind and your body.

BREATHING DEEPLY *is* MEDITATION

FEEL YOUR FEELINGS

Feel your feelings, do not ignore them. Left alone and unhealed, they will only make you calloused and afraid.

Deal with your feelings head on, the sooner the better. Take a strong, proactive stance.

Write down your thoughts and feelings in a private journal, try putting your emotions to the page.

A 2003 British Psychological Society study indicated that writing about emotions might even speed the healing of physical wounds. If journaling about pain can heal a physical injury, think about what writing might do for your broken heart. Write down your thoughts and feelings about your partner's unfaithfulness.

Tears are healthy. If they aren't coming naturally, put on some blues type music or watch a sad movie.

It's okay and healthy to laugh. Watch some funny movies or TV shows. Spend some time with people who make you smile. Life goes on in spite of heartache and unfaithful partners.

Ask all the questions you want. Talk with your partner about the infidelity. Ask the questions you need to ask and be understanding that your partner may not have all the answers just yet as to why the infidelity took place. Keep dialoguing, sharing, expressing, inviting, and listening.

See a counselor. Talking to an objective third party will help you process the situation and will stop you from being too hard on yourself.

Avoid the blame game over who or what caused the infidelity. It's just wasted energy. That includes blaming the third party. It won't change anything.

Transform your anxiety into gratitude. Gratitude transforms fear and pain into something else. When you're in angst over loss, filled with fear…name five things you're grateful for. It's a way to become present with yourself and connected. Allow yourself time to concentrate on what is good and right in your life - there is something in your life to be thankful for. Relish those things with regularity. This strategy works miracles for bringing a person out of any gloomy mood.

Take a break from your worries. Make time for some feel good activities - anything from having a cup of coffee with a friend to taking the kids to the zoo, getting a massage or playing a round of golf. Get out and about, break the routine and enjoy the adventures without relationship woes or discussions to contend with.

Learn how to relax. Just thinking about relaxing is a good thing. Saying the word 'relax' to yourself is a great thing. Actually relaxing is the best thing. Remember, it's one breath away. Tell yourself, *"I am calm" "I am safe" "I can handle this"* over and over again.

Learn the art of taking minute vacations. Anything from smelling a flower to petting an animal can help take you away for even a minute, which starts the process of feeling free.

Give to others. Kindness and charity, no matter what you feel like inside, is a win/win. Doing good, feels good. Studies show that the happiest people are ones who give the most happiness to others. When you're depressed, anxious, or stressed, there is a high degree of focus on the self. Focusing on the needs of others literally helps shift your thinking and your mood from victimhood to empowerment.

Get an ego boost. To move on from the psychological self-hatred, try some retail therapy, get a new haircut, buy some new clothes. Move on from the doldrums and make yourself feel special.

The sounds of silence. After you have done a chore, run an errand, or completed a call, take some time to sit and be — no noise, no music, nothing. Silence. It is amazing how rejuvenating this is, and also how inspiring. You never know what solution might pop into your head when you have a moment of silence to yourself.

Did YOU know?
Noise raises stress levels
Studies show that **loud noise** raises the risk **of heart attack** in both men and women

Lower the phone volume, the iPod volume, the volume of your life

Take it **one** day at a time

STRESS SUPPRESS Rx QUICK TIPS

 DON'T

- Smoke
- Procrastinate
- Sleep too much
- Overeat or eat too little
- Self-medicate with alcohol or drugs
- Use sleeping pills or tranquilizers to relax
- Withdraw from friends, family, and activities
- Fill up every minute of the day to avoid facing problems

DO

- Go for a walk
- Play with a pet
- Get a massage
- Listen to music
- Take a long bath
- Watch a comedy
- Take a yoga class
- Write in your journal
- Work in your garden
- Spend time in nature
- Curl up with a good book
- Talk to a supportive friend
- Do something for someone else
- Sweat out tension with a good workout

Getting over STRESS is different for each and every one of us. Therefore it is important to be accepting of change and to try out new techniques that you might not have thought of.

DO not discount anything -
you never know which 'trick' might work best for you

YOUR RELATIONSHIP WITH OTHERS:

Surround yourself with friends. Don't try to get through coping with unfaithfulness unaided.

Friends are your life support system, your allies, your outlet. Do not try to cope with this alone, spend time with friends and talk about everyday stuff, not just this stuff.

Don't be mistrustful of everyone - just because one person let you down does not mean everyone will. Do not let this upset cause you to become a bitter and angry person.

Set boundaries with friends and family - it's okay to say, "*No.*" Even the most well-intentioned person can become an irritation if you do not speak up. If your best friend is too forceful in their opinions and they won't listen when you say, "*I really don't want to talk about this now,*" then assign them another chore; perhaps taking care of the kids for a few hours while you spend some time alone. They want to help, but they might not know how to— so tell them!

Do NOT hang around sad people - misery might love company, but that does not do you any favors right now. You will only end up absorbing their sadness and distress, and you have enough to deal with on your own. Be sure to surround yourself with people that will uplift you.

- As much as you may feel alone right now, it is imperative that you are not.
- Make wise choices about who you surround yourself with and be firm.
- Ask for help or talk to a friend who is good at listening.
- Friends are there to help, even if they don't know it.
- Look for the silver lining, not the cloud.

MANAGING YOUR THOUGHTS AND THINKING!

Everything is so confusing -

It's hard to focus

Clarify your priorities. Write a list of what you need to get done and then do it... when you can - things can wait, and if they can't then get them done as soon as you can, but be gentle with yourself.

Do the least amount of work possible to meet your priorities. Whether it's cooking dinner for the kids or getting a report done for work, choose the simple meal and get the report done so it covers what is needed. Neither of these need to be perfect, they just need to be completed.

Give yourself permission to not make any important decisions right now. Most decisions can wait until you have sorted through the emotional mess. The relationship might be shaky, it might be over, but you do not have to decide what to do about it just yet. If you've already temporarily separated from your partner and you're worried about financial issues – then you may need to hire an attorney to get a temporary order forbidding disposal of any marital assets along with a support order if you are financially dependent. However, if you must take this route be firm with your lawyer - tell him or her that this is just for your peace of mind and that you do not plan to make any decisions soon.

I can't get the AFFAIR out of my mind!

Emotional Sex Scenario

"I got 'punched' again today. I thought I was doing really well, handling things better and not thinking about the betrayal, and then suddenly a whole deluge of emotions came flooding in as I remembered the texts and love letters my husband sent to his so called 'friend'. I feel betrayed all over again. Will I ever get over this?"

How can I stop obsessing about my partner's infidelity?

Sometimes the hardest thing to do is get through the day without obsessing.

Every little detail of the betrayal rushes through your mind, the questions without answers, the answers you don't want to hear or even imagine - did she sleep in our bed? Did he tell her our secrets? Did they really stop communicating? Are they together now? Are there more skeletons in the closet? Does my partner really love me? Am I loveable? What other lies are still waiting to be revealed? Round and round the pain-producing thoughts go. Obsessing is like having an instant replay button in your head that projects your anxiety from the past, into the future, destroying your NOW.

"Your worst enemy cannot harm you as much as your own unguarded thoughts."
The Buddha

Often your present is actually going quite well, except when you are allowing what is good to be ruined by what was, or are worrying about might be (again). What you focus on determines how you feel and the direction your actions will take. Since anxiety is the root cause of obsessions, healing from obsessions comes through reducing your anxiety and recognizing that your pain-producing, agitating thoughts are just a bunch of **stinking thinking brain noise** that's running amok.

For YOUR sanity and well-being, all these obsessive thoughts have to be stopped, and the best way to do it is to say, *"STOP!"* If the thoughts won't stop, then say, *"NO! STOP NOW!"* If they persist, then continue, *"ENOUGH! NO MORE! STOP!"*

Saying, *"STOP!"* interrupts the obsessive thought process and breaks the cycle of pain.

It is important to try to redirect your thoughts to other subjects - the kids, work, sports, something light-hearted... AWAY from the pain of the **INFIDELITY**. In fact, the best way to change your thinking is to focus on something GOOD that is happening. Something that you are grateful for right now.

If you absolutely cannot stop the 'stinking thinking' then go on a 5 Day **OBSESSION** Weaning DIET. It works like this. **Day 1.** Give yourself a time limit (no more than 5 minutes an hour) to obsess. Set an alarm - obsess all you want (for up to 5 minutes) and then STOP for the rest of the hour and refocus your attention on something positive. In the next hour, indulge yourself or postpone the session, your choice (however you forfeit the minutes, they are not cumulative). **Days 2-4:** Limit the amount of 'stinking thinking' time per hour you give yourself (e.g., Day 2 - 4 minutes, Day 3 - 3 minutes, Day 4 - 2 minutes). **Day 5:** You'll be down to no more than 1 minute an hour or LESS. **By Day 6:** You'll KNOW that you CAN control your thinking, and DO have the power to observe and refocus your thoughts.

You feel what you think
Thoughts lead to feelings that lead to behavior
Negative thinking only prolongs your suffering...

You can't control what happened,
but you can control your reaction to it

Repeat this... regularly:

"These images going round and round in my head are not real, not related to NOW, and are hurting me each time I replay them."

"This is MY mind! I am the only person who can put images or thoughts there."

"Where would I be and how would I feel if I did not allow anyone, anything or my own negative thoughts to rent space in my head right now?"

"I am in charge of my own mind. As I rule my mind and choose my thoughts, I rule my world and choose results."

*You cannot make wise life-altering decisions
If you do not look after YOUrself*

Good Things to do for YOU:

- ✓ Force yourself to eat healthy foods

- ✓ Stay on a schedule

- ✓ Sleep regular hours

- ✓ Get some exercise each day (it helps burn off some emotions)

- ✓ Drink plenty of water

- ✓ Do something that will make you laugh or smile

When we are young, we intuitively know how to calm ourselves, but we lose that ability when we grow up. Imagine you're a baby in a crib crying out and nobody comes - how do you find a way to self-soothe? I was a thumb sucker although I don't do that anymore!

Let me ask you, currently, how do you give yourself what you need? Often we do it by overeating, using substances, or distracting ourselves with things like Internet and addictions (adult thumb sucking!).

This is a good time to learn healthy ways to calm and take good care of yourself. You won't be able to fully give or receive care and love from your partner if you cannot give it to yourself.

Now is the time to HEAL.

Part 2

HEALING

"To change something, build a new model that makes the existing model obsolete."

— R. Buckminster Fuller

Although you can't go back and undo the past events, you CAN start from HERE to build a happier, more connected, responsive, and love-secure future together. The roadmap to renewed partnering lies ahead.

It's time to enter RELATIONSHIP REHAB

CHAPTER

9

REPAIR

Your Relationship is in Trouble
and You Want to Fix it

RELATIONSHIP REHAB AND HEALING

IS THERE A WAY TO REPAIR OUR RELATIONSHIP?

"What am I supposed to do? I have a constant pain in my gut. I can't even look at my husband without getting nauseous or crying. Do I continue to cook his meals? Sleep with him? He wants to play golf this weekend. I'm thinking I want to separate. I don't want a divorce, but I am ambivalent about staying and opening my heart to him again. Is there hope?"

Did YOU know?
This is a perfect OPPORTUNITY to clean the wounds of the *past* and learn new lessons for the *future*

YES, there *is* hope! Most couples I've worked with who have successfully survived and thrived after an affair more often than not, began the healing process with an overshadowing sense of ambivalence.

Of course you don't feel 100% confident or motivated. What is important is that you make a conscious choice to begin.

At the very least, you'll understand more about yourself and your relationship and with this understanding, you can make a wise and informed choice in the future.

"Life is not the way it's supposed to be. It is the way it is. The way you cope with it is what makes the difference. The event does not determine how you respond to the event - that is purely a personal matter. The way in which we respond will direct and influence the event more than the event itself."

Virginia Satir

Reworking *and* **rebuilding** *a relationship after infidelity isn't easy*

but neither is dissolving one

This is a profound opportunity to transform the damaged dynamics that led to the affair and build a stronger, more secure and lovingly conscious relationship together.

But first, I just want to make sure we are on the same page.

- ✓ You have a lot invested in your primary relationship; just chucking it is not your first choice.
- ✓ Rather than making a hasty, reactive decision based on feelings of hurt, revenge, shock or abandonment, you are each willing to let the dust settle before making major life decisions.
- ✓ You both want to commit to work through the relationship and individual issues that caused the infidelity and not call it quits with each other.

In order to salvage a relationship after an affair, the cheating partner has to give up the lover or whatever the act has been, whether it be the Internet, the physical affair or an emotional affair.

THIS IS NON-NEGOTIABLE

WHAT CAN WE DO AS A COUPLE TO SALVAGE OUR RELATIONSHIP?

For the **two** of you to work on and salvage this relationship, there have to be **two** people willing to do that. You can't do it alone; one person can't do it single-handedly.

Mutual Commitment to the process of healing is the foundational bedrock of successful Relationship Rehab and healing. It is a promise to continue investing in the relationship despite the hurt, the pain, the disappointment and yes, even the betrayal. It's about remembering the GOOD of the past, the GOOD in each other, and holding onto the big picture and relationship vision of what you want to create together from this moment forward.

It takes inner strength, determination and patience to stick it out and work through problems rather than give up. Patience is the ability to persevere and keep your heart open and hopeful when changes don't happen as quickly as you'd like. It involves grabbing each other's hand, moving away from your separate benches onto the mutual playing field and forging ahead on the same team in spite of the obstacles and with the focus of making it through and making it work.

You can get through this.
> *You can actually have deeper,*
> *more honest love on the other end of this*

Something has happened between you that, in a way, is like an earthquake shaking up your relationship to the core, and letting you start anew.

Just like rebuilding a home that's been knocked down, this time you're going to put down a stronger and more sustainable foundation to make your relationship solid, trustworthy, and supple.

It all starts with radical honesty.

It starts with the unfaithful partner being willing to make amends and understand that they don't want to cheat ever again. For the one who has been betrayed, it takes the ability (once you move through your feelings) to understand and forgive. It takes a commitment by both of you to reprioritize your relationship as #1 in significance in your life. And, it takes living in TRUTH.

To repair the relationship and rebuild trust, it's important that you and your partner talk openly and honestly about what happened and how it happened. Rather than relating like a detective investigating a crime, it is important to approach this discussion as two people who want to understand each other better. It's time to be radically honest about who you are, what you want, and what you need.

The truth is you have nothing to lose
and everything to gain

"View all problems as challenges. Look upon the negatives that arise as opportunities to learn and grow. Don't run from them, condemn yourself, or bury your burden in saintly silence. Have a problem? Great! More grist for the mill. Rejoice, dive in and investigate."

Bhante Henepola Gunaratana -
Mindfulness in Plain English

ARE YOU REALLY READY TO REPAIR AND REBUILD?

✅ For the UNFAITHFUL PARTNER

It is important for you to understand the pain you've caused and the damage your affair has created. Be empathetic. Your partner is probably going through post-traumatic stress; feeling shocked, confused, angry, hurt and highly sensitive. You have to be patient as your partner moves through their grief. Be ready to **continually** apologize, ask for forgiveness and say, *"I'm sorry I hurt you"* - once is not enough.

In order to heal your relationship, you will have to stand strong and resolute in your conviction to make the relationship work, no matter what the obstacle and in spite of whatever or however your partner's reaction may initially manifest itself. The more you hold onto the vision and commitment to genuinely LOVE, the quicker the relationship will calm down and feel safer. For a while, you may be the only one holding the belief that *'we will get through this'* until your partner gets back on board and is ready to forgive and trust again.

ARE YOU *REALLY* READY TO HEAL AND REBUILD?

- ❓ Have you ended your affair?
- ❓ Have you fully withdrawn, grieved, and let go of your lover?
- ❓ Is this a pattern for you? Have you had multiple affairs?
- ❓ Have you figured out WHY you had the affair(s)?
- ❓ Do you truly take responsibility and deeply regret your lies, deception and betrayal and sincerely want to make amends?
- ❓ Has your apology been given, believed and accepted?
- ❓ Have you figured out WHY you want to come home?
- ❓ Are you willing to do whatever it takes to earn your partner's trust back and rebuild your relationship?
- ❓ Are you ready to be faithful?

Be prepared - this will be a long road

 For the BETRAYED PARTNER

In order to begin the process of healing and rebuilding your relationship with your unfaithful partner, you have to re-channel your energy and focus from what has happened to you, how bad you feel, and how betrayed you are, and instead start spending time honestly looking at who you are and what you want.

- ❓ "What is it that I want? "
- ❓ "Who am I now that this has happened?"
- ❓ "What are my needs in this relationship?"
- ❓ "What kind of relationship do I want to have?"

This is an opportunity to rediscover **your** needs, desires and VOICE.

There is no status quo anymore about what kind of relationship you want. Challenge the old rules, roles, and reasons for being together. This is a new beginning - what are you willing to give to create the relationship you want?

For REAL healing to happen in your relationship, it has to start within. You have to get to a place inside where you are strong enough to forgive and ready to trust again...yourself, your partner, and your partnership. You have to be willing to MOVE ON from the pain, heal the wounds of betrayal and start the process of forgiveness. Because the first step to really healing the relationship is allowing yourself to forgive in order to build trust again. Trust of yourself, trust in your partner's reliability and faithfulness, and trust that the relationship can and will survive.

ARE YOU *REALLY* READY TO HEAL AND REBUILD?

- Have you started your own soul-searching, hand-holding, wound-licking, need exploring, and self-nurturing work on yourself?
- Have you explored your options i.e. (staying or choosing to leave) and how each would affect your life? Have you decided to stay for the right reasons?
- Have you told your truth, shared your feelings, cleared the air yet?
- Do you want to forgive your partner and build a better relationship?
- Underneath all this chaos, do you still love your partner?
- Do you want to save your relationship?

✔ For BOTH PARTNERS

To heal, you need to both figure out what problems in your relationship led to the affair.

There are reasons the affair happened, and NOW is the time to find out what they are.

It's important that both of you sit down and discuss:

- ➲ What exactly caused the affair.
- ➲ The role it played in your life, and...
- ➲ What pre-existing problems, behaviors and attitudes led to the affair happening.

Without identifying why the affair happened, you're greatly increasing the risk that there will be a repeat performance in the future.

To objectively identify what went wrong, you have to both stop blaming the betrayer's action as the cause of your unhappiness and *each recognize* the parts you played in the affair happening in the first place.

You and your partner created your relationship together and your current life and relationship problems were created by the two of you.

TOGETHER, as a team, you can FACE the weaknesses and change the temperature, intimacy, and emotional climate between you. Begin to take concrete steps to strengthen that relationship and see what develops.

Now is the time to get down and get real. Put your cards on the table. Get the real issues and associated feelings out in the open where they can be addressed, analyzed, discussed, and worked through.

Let's get to work...

RELATIONSHIP CHECK POINT

Are you aware of the role the affair played in your life?

Here are some questions to dialogue about. You should both have an opportunity to speak freely and calmly to the other. It's important to not get too worked up, no matter what you each say, and to take a break if things get heated during your discussion. (*See more about this in the Communication chapter)

For the unfaithful: Did it fill a void? Was it a distraction? Did you use it as an escape from boredom? Was it simply an opportunity that got out of hand? Was it a quick sexual fling with no meaning? Or was it an emotionally meaningful connection with another?

For the betrayed: Did it get your partner off your back? Did it keep your relationship at a safe distance? Did it give you time and space to focus on other things? Or did it just make you angry, frustrated or disappointed?

What relationship vulnerabilities existed that led to the affair? Often an affair is a symptom of a problem rather than the cause. When infidelity occurs, it's easy to fall prey to putting the focus on the affair rather than the entire picture of why it happened. Were you both committed but had no real intimacy? Was it the result of an emotional disconnect? Were you living separate lives and separate schedules? Was there a serious communication breakdown? Unexpressed resentment? Too many life stressors? Differing needs or values? Unclear attitudes about what an affair is?

Are you each willing to take responsibility for why and how the infidelity happened? In attempting to assign responsibility for the infidelity, the hurt partner tends to blame the betrayer saying *"YOU did this to US. You cheated, I didn't. Don't blame me. It's YOUR responsibility."*

The unfaithful partner tends to blame their partner and say in some fashion... *"You weren't there for me. You drove me to this. If you were a better partner, then this wouldn't have happened."*

Are you ready to stop pointing fingers at each other and accept a rightful share of the responsibility for the affair?

Are you and your partner willing to change the relationship dynamics that led one of you to have an affair?

If there was a physical affair, have you both been tested for STDs?

Are you both willing to do what it takes to work on the relationship and make it work? Can you repent and repair? Are you prepared to become an open book? Will you prioritize relationship rebuilding into the #1 position of importance?

"The fact that we are here and that I speak these words is an attempt to break that silence and bridge some of those differences between us, for it is not difference which immobilizes us, but silence. And there are so many silences to be broken."

Audre Lorde

CHAPTER

10

COMMUNICATION

Essential Skills for Your
Relationship First Aid Kit

RELATIONSHIP REHAB AND HEALING

Communication is the process of exchanging information with one another. Everything we do and say, as well as what we do NOT do or say, transmits information.

What and how we **communicate** is the way we know and are known by each other. Few experiences are more gratifying than expressing yourself, saying something that is deep and personal and having it heard, received, and understood by your partner. From this, intimacy, closeness and bonding is continually renewed.

When we don't feel heard or understood, we don't feel seen or loved. This leads to emotional disengagement and **communication** breakdown.

Many relationships become vulnerable to affairs when the **communication** breaks down and the emotional space between them grows. Most relationship problems and complaints, whether it be about sex, money, raising children, jealousy... all source back to a breakdown in **communication**.

Communication is extremely important in times of stress and emergency.

Without **communication** we are left in the dark where our fears are given strength, our doubts are given power and our trust is always fragile.

In order to build a stronger and better relationship after such a devastating event, it is imperative to **communicate** clearly, honestly, and frequently.

Emotional Sex Scenario:

"I totally agree about letting the entire truth out. That's what I asked my wife to do...tell me everything! Most of what she told me was very hurtful, but I needed to hear it so that I'd know what I was dealing with. It's been three months now...the first week was really bad, but after that it got easier. We talked a lot and held on to each other for comfort and support. We're coming out of this stronger than ever, from romance to commitment to friendship to realizing that we don't want to live without each other. Our love is so much deeper now than it ever was. It's just too bad that we had to go through this situation to restore the love we always knew was there, but I guess we took for granted.

I have to be honest with you, at the beginning of the affair discovery, I didn't even think that a counselor could help us get out of the mess that we were in, but somehow we are talking it through and working it out. My wounds are not totally healed, but it's just a matter of time because I know that I have my soul mate and my best friend by my side. Hanging in there and working through this, I now know how much she loves me, and I love her. Hopefully your wounds are healing quickly as well and you'll be able to re-establish whatever was missing from your relationship. Communicate, talk and share everything that you can with each other... that's truly one of the secrets of a long, happy relationship."

The most important part of the healing process is finding a way to communicate effectively again, or perhaps for the first time.

Many couples don't have the ability to calmly and effectively communicate without becoming angry or letting their judgment become clouded.

It's time NOW to learn and apply effective communication.

"Behind the need to communicate is the need to share
Behind the need to share is the need to be understood."

Leo Rosten

RELATIONSHIP FIRST AID KIT

Language for Lovers: Skilled Speaking, Excellent Hearing

What is effective communication in a relationship?

It's very simple.

> *The message sent
> is the message being received*

What you say to your partner is actually heard by your partner.

"The single biggest problem in communication is the illusion that it has taken place."

George Bernard Shaw

Is the message sent, the message received?
Are you being heard?   Are you listening?

A couples quick communication quiz

1. When you express yourself do you know you are being heard?

2. Do you both actively seek to understand each other?

3. Are you open to each other's thoughts and feelings?

4. Do you feel comfortable sharing with your partner?

5. When issues arise, do you face them as a team?

If you answered NO to any of these questions, you and your partner need to work on **communicating** more effectively with each other so that your relationship can move forward successfully.

A question I am often asked is...

How can I get my partner to listen and understand me?

It's not only WHAT you say, it's also HOW you say it.

HOW you express your needs, desires, and requests for change can mean the difference between finding resolution or starting a fight.

Think... DELIVERY **and PRESENTATION**

DELIVERY AND PRESENTATION:

How to eliminate blame-filled, character assassination and accusatory language...

1. State your positive intention - *"I feel like this issue is coming between us and getting in the way. I hope that by sharing this information with you that we can work together in resolving it. I want to feel closer to you again."*

Did YOU know?

Successful conversations do not necessarily mean getting your way

2. Describe the situation and the behavior that upsets you - Be as specific and objective as possible. *"When I come home, and you don't come to greet me, say hello or give me a kiss..."* This specifically describes the behavior which is bothering you versus *"When I come home and you ignore me"* which would usually create an immediate defensive reaction.

3. Express your feelings and thoughts - Most feelings we experience are the result of what we think, believe, interpret, and tell ourselves. Our thoughts lead to feelings that lead to our reactions and behaviors. Start with what you are feeling... *I feel_____ (angry, sad, scared)* and then add the thought behind it... *because I (believe, think, am telling myself) that_____(You don't love me. You're leaving me. You're going to cheat on me again.).* When you recognize and own the thoughts that are activating your feelings, it shifts you out of the blame mode, frees your partner from being on the defensive, and empowers both of you to get down to the real issues and changes needed.

4. Specify your wants and what you'd like to change - Ask specifically for an observable change - *"When you come home I'd like it if, before going upstairs, you'd come and find me, give me a hug, and say hi. Are you willing to do that?"*

A successful conversation allows you to express your thoughts, feelings and/or concerns in a way that is heard and understood. It also means consciously listening and seeking to understand what is being said to you.

This kind of communicating takes practice but the results are well worth it.

4 TIPS

for PEACEFUL, COOPERATIVE and SKILLFUL
CONVERSING

1. "I" Speak... own it:

- Use "I" statements such as *"I need, I feel, I want, I desire."*

- Avoid placing blame with you-oriented words or "you" statements such as: *"You need to." "Your problem is." "You're not."*

- The key is to make your partner aware, not wrong. *"This issue is important to me. I would like to talk to you about it. I promise not to yell or get upset."*

- Practice using "I" statements and you'll notice an immediate improvement in your dialogue.

2. Tone and Body Language:

- If you're talking calmly and lovingly, you have a far better chance of keeping your partner's attention on what you are saying.

- When someone starts talking really loudly or aggressively, pointing fingers, tensing up, the receiver instinctively goes on the defensive and puts protective walls up.

- You can't expect anyone to listen fully when they feel they are being laid into.

- When you hold an attitude of **cooperation versus competition** (e.g.,*"we're in this together"*, *"we're a team"*), your body relaxes and your tone automatically becomes kinder, gentler, and calmer.

3. Ask for Feedback - Invite Discussion:

- One surefire way of knowing you are being heard is asking for feedback.

- *"What do you think of this?" "Do you understand where I'm coming from?"*

- Feedback also allows you to reaffirm (or resend) any important messages that may have been overlooked or missed.

4. Each Partner has a Turn:

- Turn around is fair play. Remember to take turns having your say and being heard. That means giving each other your full attention and listening without interruption.

When it comes to relationship problems and issues of the heart, sloppy listening just doesn't cut it

we need to step up our game
and open up our heart and our ears

BASIC LISTENING FOR LOVERS

Turn in. Tune in. Take it in.

Generally speaking
you aren't learning much when your lips are moving

Listening takes work.

Sometimes the hardest part is resisting the urge to push (whether it be pushing your point or pushing away) and instead, staying relaxed, present, and available to hear.

What you've got to do is take a deep breath and repeat, *"I love my partner. I'm going to listen and I'm not going to react."*

Listening is not just about hearing what your partner is saying. When you truly LISTEN it lets your partner know that you are taking them in and that they are being heard, known, accepted and understood.

This is literally **LOVE** in action.

Wordlessly you communicate
"I hear you. I get you. I receive you as you are. I love you."

Having our words, feelings, and thoughts heard, taken in and received feels like LOVE on the deepest level of our being.

Listening while other people are talking tends to be a selective process in most conversations.

We have trained ourselves to take in just enough to get by and/or get out of the conversation.

Truthfully, sometimes it's hard to listen to your partner's pain, complaints, or unhappiness without getting defensive, wanting to fix it, or shut down to avoid the guilt.

Typically, when your partner is speaking and you are becoming uncomfortable, your mind may wander and become distracted, or you may become carried away in the tide of your own reactions or defense preparation.

However, when trying to build or repair trust it helps to see and understand the situation from your partner's point of view.

Be committed to seeing your partner's perspective and HEAR the disguised **heart call**

Try to understand what your partner is asking for and why your partner is so upset.

Listen for and acknowledge his or her feelings and perspective of the situation.

You don't have to totally AGREE with your partner's version or facts, but let them know that you hear what they are saying and GET why they are hurt.

COMMUNICATION • 177

HEARING YOUR PARTNER'S (DISGUISED) HEART CALL

Usually whatever we are fighting about can be boiled down to one of the following bottom lines:

"I don't feel loved."

"I don't feel heard."

"I don't feel understood."

However this call may be being communicated (sometimes disguised and distorted in fearful, crabby, angry, frustrated, blaming, annoying, and less than satisfying ways), it's important to recognize that this is your partner's heart calling for love, attention, reassurance, and/or approval.

Feeling safe with one another comes from trusting that we are known, loved, and accepted as we are.

To successfully navigate and resolve whatever you are fighting about, you have to find within yourself the creativity, patience, understanding, and inner security to stop pushing away or against your partner and instead start leaning IN saying -

"I'm here."

"I'm willing to hear you."

"I'm interested in what you have to say."

"Let's work this out."

LISTENING IS LOVE IN ACTION

Listening is not only being a receptive ear, it is giving feedback to your partner.

It's showing that you understand their position and are not judging them for it.

Do not interrupt. Be interested.

Ask questions related to what your partner is talking about..

Encourage them to share their truth without fear — *"Tell me more."* *"I would like to hear more about what you think and feel." "I'm here to talk about it with you."*

Let your body show that you are listening and interested - *nodding, saying yes, uh-huh, leaning in and making eye contact.*

After your partner has shared, let your partner know that you've truly heard what they've had to say.

Respond in kindness, without defense.

What a powerful and profound experience it is when both partners have the opportunity to share and be listened to in this way.

"To listen well is as powerful a means of communication as to talk well."

John Marshall

WAYS TO KEEP CONVERSATION (& LOVE) OPEN & FLOWING

Ask Questions - be interested

"Tell me how you feel about..." / "Why are you so upset?" / "I want to understand." / "What can I do to make things better?"

Clarify - make sure you are receiving what is being sent

Let your partner know that you are trying to understand. Make sure to listen for the relevant details...

Summarize - let your partner know that the message sent was the message received

"This is what I heard you say..."

Validate - I am on your side, we are a team

"I can imagine how upsetting this is for you. I am glad we are trying to figure this out."

"We have two ears and one mouth so that we can listen twice as much as we speak."

Epictetus (Greek Philosopher)

BODY LANGUAGE

WHAT IS YOUR BODY SAYING?

Body language signals show your partner whether or not you are tuned in, present, and listening.

Your *eye contact, facial expressions, tone of voice,* and *body gestures* demonstrate your interest, attitude, and openness.

When your partner feels heard and understood they are more likely to...

quiet down

forgive you

feel closer to you

listen to your side

Keep in mind that the minute your partner starts saying something you don't want to hear, your shoulders will tense and your instinct will likely be to leave or end the conversation.

Breathe and say, *"I'm staying here. I love my partner. I'm going to take deep breaths and listen."*

Repeat as needed.

Staying mindful of your body and conscious of what it is saying is essential to effective listening and communication.

Did YOU know?

Women *tend to make sounds like "uh-huh," "hmmm" and "ahhhhhh" which show the talker they are listening. Body gestures include shaking their head, making eye contact, and showing interest.*

Men *are more likely to remain silent and stoic. If you are the silent type, get into the habit of giving non-verbal feedback to your mate so that your partner won't have to wonder, "Am I being heard and understood?"*

A RELAXED BODY ALLOWS FOR AN OPEN MIND

When listening, sit and face your partner maintaining an open body posture.

Keep your *eyes* in contact and stay aware of your breathing. Our facial *expressions* tend to convey what we are feeling at the moment. Be mindful of what your *face* is saying. Be prepared to counter expressions of indifference or disagreement by reminding yourself that your job is to **listen** and support, not to judge or advise.

And don't forget to watch your *breathing*. When agitated, our breathing becomes quick and shallow. If you notice this happening, take long deep breaths. This focuses the mind and relaxes the body, allowing you to return to a **receptive** (instead of reactive) state.

DO:

- → Face your partner
- → Keep your eyes in contact
- → Stay aware of your breathing
- → Maintain an open posture - uncross your arms, your heart and your mind
- → Keep yourself open and aware and present by remembering that LISTENING is LOVE

We all need to be listened to and understood.

Listening is one of the kindest, most loving things you can do for and with your partner

Now armed with better heart-hearing and communication skills, it is important to realize that your relationship will face challenges.

The secret is DO NOT PANIC or OVERREACT when the inevitable storms arrive.

There are always tests, trials and turbulence to navigate.

The stronger the team the easier the resolve will be when issues arise...

STORM WATCH

EMOTIONAL DISCONNECTS, TROUBLE MAKERS AND LOVE SQUASHERS
DISAGREEMENTS, POWER STRUGGLES, FIGHTS, CONFLICTS

Why do our disagreements turn into ugly arguments?

A disagreement can easily evolve into a full-blown argument when our heart's call for love, attention, and approval is unheard and unmet by our partner. That's when the call for love shifts into a 'who's right, who's wrong' battle with full trumpets blaring. The energy of our needs and desires transmute into finger-pointing daggers of blame. The more we try to prove our point, the louder the return protest becomes. Nothing gets resolved and the feelings of aloneness and separation escalate from there.

Disagreements can actually be HELPFUL to your relationship.

Disagreements force each of us to stretch our perspective and sometimes leave our comfort zone. Successfully wrestling through our differences can lead us into a deeper, more enduring love with our partner. As Victor Hugo said, *"The greatest happiness in life is the conviction that we are loved - loved for ourselves, or rather, **loved in spite of ourselves.**"* Learning to tenaciously hold onto love with an open heartedness as we resolve our differences helps us to step through the illusion of who we want our partner to be and expands our acceptance and love of who they *really* are.

What can my partner and I do if we can't resolve our disagreement?

Sometimes, when we're embroiled in a disagreement, we get stuck. All creative solutions fly out the window and all we feel is hardness and rigidity. The most important agreement to have when you are disagreeing or stuck in a power struggle is that you won't yell or berate each other, and that you will be nice and treat each other with the utmost respect, no matter what.

Feeling upset is contagious.

Stress challenges your ability to successfully communicate. When either one of you are feeling or acting agitated, withdrawn, attacked or frightened, you automatically look, hear, touch and react differently than you do when you feel 'just right'. The conversation may quickly spiral out of control as your hearts go deaf and you fall into defensive/protective/knee-jerk reactive patterns. These are times in relationship when it is best to WAIT before you act.

Emotional Sex Scenario:

"It was me, not him, that couldn't get past it. I swung from one extreme to another - one morning I would wake up and think that I was going to try to be receptive to him and work on our relationship, and then by afternoon I would have visions of them together sitting on our couch, sipping our wine, playing music from my iPod, and it would ruin my mood and my day. I swung from being the accommodating wife who wanted to work it out to a furious, impulsive person who would lash out and say and do things that would harm our attempts to save the marriage. And, in the back of my mind, I was thinking 'no wonder he cheated on you, you're being awful,' but I just couldn't stop myself."

❌ How can I stop myself from yelling at my partner?

- ➡ You must have an iron-clad agreement NOT to yell at each other...
- ➡ If you raise your voice, apologize and lower it again...
- ➡ Say these words, out loud to each other -
- ➡ "No matter how upset I feel, I will try to be nice to you and do whatever I can to avoid yelling and screaming."
- ➡ If you cannot control your anger and the volume of your voice, then get up, take a time out...
- ➡ Stomp it out. Write it out. Breathe it out... until the fury dissipates.

❌ How can I stop my partner from yelling at me?

- ➡ When they yell, stay quiet, do not try to defend yourself.
- ➡ As they get to the end of their rant, ask them not to shout anymore.
- ➡ Let them know you are hearing them and they can express themselves calmly.
- ➡ Acknowledge their side of the discussion, and then ask what can be done to make it okay.
- ➡ If their anger is out of control, then get up and walk away with a promise to return when things have calmed down.

Don't shout.

TALK

COMMUNICATION AND STRESS - NOT GOOD BEDFELLOWS

Stress can cause communication problems and damage relationships:

✅ It's easy to push each other's buttons. Fear attracts fear. When one partner is stressed and upset, it can easily trigger the other's upset - leading to a communication and emotional disconnect.

✅ When you are overwhelmed by stress, your awareness, presence and ability to listen to your partner - and to yourself - is greatly impaired.

✅ Stress can re-awaken and activate the negative ghosts of past behaviors and reactions, adding to the upset of the moment.

"People are lonely
because they build walls instead of bridges."
Joseph F. Newton

Communicating when BOTH of you are out of balance, will make matters worse.
Whatever the issue...
Whatever the circumstance...

⊗ DO NOT:

- ➲ Do NOT demean, name call or threaten
- ➲ Do NOT generalize - "You always..." or "You never..."
- ➲ Do NOT push your partner's sore or sensitive buttons
- ➲ Do NOT roll your eyes, smirk or talk under your breath
- ➲ Do NOT bring up a multitude of unresolved issues at once
- ➲ Do NOT forget that words do matter - avoid saying things you will regret later
- ➲ Do NOT try to win by digging up painful or embarrassing information from the past
- ➲ Do NOT ask accusatory questions that start the conversation off on the wrong foot... Try not to start with "Why..."

When hearts go DEAF, talking to or from a DEAF heart is a waste of words, especially when you are trying to explain, prove, win over, get your partner to see your point of view, or win back your partner's love.

At least ONE of you MUST calm, center and restore your balance in order to keep the heart in the conversation alive and beating.

Take a breath.   Take a pause.
Take off your armor.

Catch yourself in the moment.

Recognize the stress imbalance in yourself.

KNOW that it's never too late to SHIFT and REBUILD the moment.

* The return to closeness, agreement and good feeling, connected love is not going to happen until you let down the shields, melt your body armor, 'un-guard' your heart and hear the underlying calls for love - both your own and your partner's.

If it gets out of hand -

CALL FOR A TIME OUT to...

....HEAR **LOVE**'S CALL
become present
MELT YOUR ARMOR

Here is a great way to begin to melt your own armor, breathe life back into your heart, and open up to feel the love inside you.

The following process is very powerful to do together as a couple, but if your partner isn't ready yet, then the most important thing you can do is to lovingly become present within yourself.

First, (this may be the hardest part) **STOP** doing whatever you are doing that is fueling the fires of aggravation and aggression - let go of any and all agendas, defensive posturing, cases to build, the shame, blame, or that *"I just have one more important thing to say"* that's inside you burning to be spoken or screamed.

Look at each other and wait until you really SEE your partner.

Then say, *"All is well. This obstacle that we are encountering is here to strengthen our love and acceptance. We may be a little stuck right now but we'll get through this! I love you."*

Then take a 15 minute break making a promise to return.

Take some deep breaths and on the exhale, let out a sound or sigh that physically helps you to release tension from your body. Begin to imagine and feel the air of your breath as it enters and leaves through your heart area/center of your chest. Think of a calming word, such as *love, peace, relax, joy,* and slowly breathe the energy of the word in and out, saying to yourself. *"I'm breathing in... love. I'm breathing out... love".*

Do this until it feels true and your body begins to relax and center.

Notice...

- How do I resist love?
- Where am I holding tension?
- Am I feeling connected or disconnected?
- What am I saying to myself and/or out loud that creates separation?

Breathe deeply into the place in your body that most strongly holds your sense of separation and resistance to love. Lovingly and with full acceptance, breathe the energy of your chosen word into that place. The goal isn't to make it go away or even change. It's about honoring, accepting and listening softly.

And then ponder these questions...

- How would love respond?
- If I could transform this moment, how would I want it to be?
- If I had a choice would I choose loving connection or lonely separation?
- What is the most productive, relationship enhancing thing I am capable of doing in this moment?

The moment you stop action and take a step back is the moment you begin to move from polarization back into communion.

When ready, return to your partner and ask....

- What do you need?
- What makes you feel most safe?
- What makes you feel most loved?
- How can I support you in achieving what you need?

THIS IS AN OPPORTUNITY FOR GROWTH & HEALING

Remember you have a choice.

Disagreements and conflict can be a road to ruin OR a path to deeper love and security in your relationship.

It takes two willing partner's remembering to say YES to love and holding hands to work it through.

Most of the time, whatever is pushing your buttons and activating a strong reaction is usually a reflection of your own unresolved wounds or belief systems that are silently screaming for attention and healing.

So, pay attention to where you lose your balance, go into automatic reactivity and literally give the power of your well being away.

The challenge becomes a blessing when you use it as a catalyst for self awareness, a call to heal, and a springboard into a new, mature, balanced way of communicating and loving.

Reconnection can literally be just one emotional heartbeat away - it involves taking a pause, becoming present, and opening to attune and commune in the spirit of curiosity, compassion and clemency.

"Love one another and you will be happy.
It's as simple and as difficult as that."
Michael Leunig

BIGGER STORMS & STRUGGLES -

POWER STRUGGLES
and the need to be right

What is a Power Struggle?

A power struggle occurs when being right is more important than being connected and in love. Basically, it's when union and communion is discarded for righteous triumph. If you and your partner both feel that yours is the only correct solution then chances are, you are in a power struggle.

Usually power struggles have little to do with what you are actually talking about, and everything to do with how each feels about their place and position in the relationship. When there has been an affair, the betrayed partner may continually use the hurt and damage that the affair has caused to wield power, emotional concession and attention - they use it as a way to control.

An argument could begin over something innocuous - where to eat, what movie to see, being late, who was supposed to pick up what, when this or that was supposed to occur... but ends up being a referendum on the relationship as a whole.

The best way to avoid power struggles is to maintain an open dialogue with your partner; one in which each side feels free to express themselves and open to compromise.

It sounds simple but it is rarely easy.

Eventually, one party will feel slighted or under-appreciated and the desire to reaffirm their place and value will manifest. It is important to recognize and combat this... *as a team.*

Power struggles are poison
to a healthy, open relationship

How can I tell if I am in Power Struggle mode?

Do a quick self-assessment:

- ➤ Does this feel like a contest?
- ➤ Is the anger quickly escalating?
- ➤ Does the idea of not winning seem totally unacceptable?
- ➤ Can you not see any validity in your partner's point of view?
- ➤ Do you feel your partner is being purposely dense or obtuse?
- ➤ Is the point you're making more important than a discussion?
- ➤ Are you positive you are right regardless of inconvenient facts?
- ➤ Do you feel your partner should "Just shut up and do/act/listen?"
- ➤ Can you listen to your partner's point of view without interruption?
- ➤ Are you ignoring your partner and just waiting for your turn to talk?
- ➤ Does the idea of compromise or failing to convince make you angry?
- ➤ Do you resort to personal attacks or unfair assessments to get your way?
- ➤ Do you feel that you're absolutely right and your partner is absolutely wrong?

If you answered YES to one or more of these questions, you are in or on the way to a power struggle with your partner.

When you become stuck in know-it-all, *'my way or the highway'*, righteous, blaming, unbending, *'I'm right you're wrong'* thinking, it's a pretty good indicator that you both are in a power struggle.

The usual partner behavioral response to this kind of deluge is to freeze, run away, or explode with anxiety and anger.

This attitude drains the blood and life force out of shared love and creates separation and a lose/lose situation.

All behaviors connected to power struggles exhibit a resistance to love.

Angry, harsh words and actions can spread damage quicker than lighter fuel on dry timber. Before you know it, the words flame out of control and cause havoc and devastation.

You stop listening, become defensive, arm up, and feel overtly protective about your position. All that is important is winning. Winning a disagreement using fear tactics such as: intimidation, finger pointing, overwhelming the opposition with anger, shutting them up, shutting down, or walking out and leaving may give us a temporary sense of *'I'm RIGHT-fullness'*, but the victory is hollow and short-lived.

No **surrender**. No **LOVE**.

How do I avoid being in a power struggle with my partner?

The best way to avoid being in a power struggle is to realize that even if you win the battle, you lose the war.

If one of you has a problem, it's a WE problem, not a ME problem.

If one partner is stuck and polarized in opposition, then there is a WE problem.

You can meet and match fear with fear, or you can hold the heart of the relationship in your arms and calm your partner.

Treat your partner as your best friend. Listen and find that place of mutual agreement, because the truth is neither one of you is 100% right and neither one of you is 100% wrong.

The task at hand is finding a way to move away from the energy of competition (me vs. you) to cooperation (we are a team).

Change your focus from looking for what's wrong, to searching for what's right—a place you agree with what your partner is saying. Start there.

"Try to see it my way,
Do I have to keep on talking till I
can't go on?

While you see it your way,
Run the risk of knowing that our love may
soon be gone."
John Lennon, Paul McCartney

Take a breath.   Take a pause.
Take off your armor.

And ask yourself.....

Do I want to be RIGHT
*Or do I want to be **HAPPY**?*

- ➲ Why do I need to be right?

- ➲ Is sticking to my position that important?

- ➲ If this was my best friend how would I
  behave?

- ➲ Is there room to lighten up and relax
  about this?

- ➲ What would it be like if I chose to be
  the generous one?

in a moment it can all change for the worse...
or for the **better**

Remind yourself that this is an opportunity to grow and learn.

Repeat after me...

"As distant as I feel from my partner in the moment, *I instead choose to* **remember a moment of closeness and begin to breathe that consciousness in**."

"I locate the areas of tension in my body, and reassure myself that all is well, this is temporary, and that we'll get through it. I realize that whatever I am feeling, believing, experiencing is generated by fear not love."

"When I'm in fear I isolate and self-protect, when I'm in love I flow and want to connect. *I HAVE A CHOICE!*"

"*I choose* to change my mind, stop reacting, and change the moment."

"Between stimulus and response there is a space. In that space is our power to choose our response. In our response lies our growth and our freedom."

Victor Frankl

PRACTICAL SOLUTIONS FOR RESOLVING POWER STRUGGLES:

⊗ Stay flexible.

⊗ Set aside the issue for a moment.

⊗ Talk about how it feels to be stuck.

⊗ Validate your partner's perspective.

⊗ Find a place of mutual agreement and work from there.

⊗ Take one issue at a time. Break the problem into smaller pieces.

⊗ Affirm and reaffirm to yourself and each other that you'll get through this.

⊗ Try to understand your partner's point of view. Listen and let them know what you've heard.

⊗ Remember to keep coming home to your body by consciously connecting to your breath and breathing.

"If you are going through hell –

KEEP GOING"

Winston Churchill

CHAPTER

11

TRUST

is a 2-way street

Without TRUST You Cannot Have a
MEANINGFUL, INTIMATE CONNECTION

RELATIONSHIP REHAB AND HEALING

HOW CAN I TRUST MY PARTNER TO NOT CHEAT AGAIN?

Now that the trust has been broken you have to move forward together with a new, shared, ongoing commitment to **'responsible honesty'** if your relationship is going to survive and succeed.

Trust is a by-product of steadfast reliability, mutual accountability, close connection, and open, truthful communication with each other.

Did YOU know?

The response to infidelity varies greatly with gender -
MEN are less trusting than WOMEN

For the betrayed, restoring the bond of trust comes from...

... knowing that your partner has severed all ties with the third party, is able to admit their mistake, is dedicated to the recovery process, and committed to do the work necessary to repair their relationship with you.

...rebuilding trust in yourself - moving from self-protect mode into understanding and learning mode. It involves trusting your own instincts again, staying awake, alert, and self-aware.

Be aware.

Be conscious.

This does not mean you are *paranoid...*

it means you are *present*.

REGAINING TRUST:

TRUST IS LIKE FAITH - YOU HAVE TO KEEP RENEWING IT

FOCUS ON THE POSITIVE.

It helps to think about all of the things your partner is trying to do to make things right again and to remember all the things he/she did that were right and good during your relationship.

YOU FEEL WHAT YOU THINK - SO, CHANGE YOUR THINKING

"It is our mind, and that alone, that chains us or sets us free."

Dilgo Khyentse Rinpoche

➲ When you are taken by surprise, feel vulnerable and hurt by your partner's cheating, your fear may put you on guard thereafter. If you don't make a conscious choice to rebuild trust, forgive and move on, you will find yourself becoming imprisoned by your fear, believing if you let down your guard, you and your relationship will be betrayed again.

➲ The work at hand is to let go of the belief that a painful event in your past can predict a painful event in your future. The difference between your past and your future is that now your eyes are open, and you are working together to build a stronger, more honest and loving foundation for your partnership to stand upon.

➲ A big key to healing is not about changing your partner but changing the conflicting, negative thoughts in YOUR mind that create a boomerang of emotional pain, anxiety, distress, and love disconnect.

REGAINING TRUST -
FOR THE DECEIVER

Trust is easy to lose...
and hard to regain

Emotional Sex Scenario

"I invented so many stories to explain my whereabouts and the additional expenses I was incurring. I had to keep a separate calendar to keep all the lies straight."

When there is infidelity, lies are part of the territory, especially when the affair enters the physical realm. Often affairs cost money, so stories about the extra expenses showing up on your credit card, or cash disappearing from your account have to be accounted for.

Often it's the lies, secrecy and deception that end up feeling more painful than the act of infidelity itself and are what haunt, hurt, and destroy TRUST the most.

If you are the deceiver, you will need to show that you clearly understand what your partner has felt and experienced, and you need to prove (over and over) that you are truly sorry, willing to change and work on earning their trust once again, no matter what it takes.

BE PATIENT - BE KIND
IT TAKES TIME

Your partner has to feel safe in order to risk being vulnerable again

- ➲ **Rebuilding trust requires** an *understanding* from you.

- ➲ **Rebuilding trust requires** *patience* that your partner may rightfully be suspicious and actively questioning your every move for quite awhile.

- ➲ **Rebuilding trust requires** you to honestly *answer* questions that may be thrown at you seemingly out of the blue, following through with actions that match your words and understanding that any reminder or replay of the original injury may conjure up a similar reaction in the present.

- ➲ **Rebuilding trust requires** you to willingly be *accountable* for your whereabouts.

Emotional Sex Scenario:

"When I was having my affair, I'd often arrive home late. Now that the affair has ended, I make a point to get home early. But yesterday I got stuck in traffic and arrived home late. No matter how consistent I've been, this one little tardiness triggered a full blown activation of suspicion, doubt, anger and fear in my partner. Will her distrust ever end?"

In order to have true intimacy (*into-me-see*) you will have to EARN the trust back.

Your words, deeds and actions MUST convey *"You are SAFE with me. I'm HERE. I love you. WE matter. YOU are important."*

Be patient. Be resolute.

TRUST IN YOUR PARTNERSHIP

REBUILDING TRUST BY REBUILDING YOUR CREDIBILITY

Promises are made and promises are kept

After the apologies, the expression of feelings and the sharing of thoughts, one of the important ways you show your seriousness, reliability, and accountability is to be a person of your word and by keeping the promises you make, come hell or high water.

When one partner has been betrayed, it is important that the other partner (the betrayer) make unequivocal promises about their future behavior and be accountable and resolute in their follow through. For example, your promise to be faithful may involve actions of regularly checking in and reassuring your partner that you are where you're supposed to be, doing what you're supposed to be doing. In other words, being predictable, reliable, and available for contact at any time.

CONSISTENT ACTIONS AND FOLLOW THROUGH THAT MATCH WORDS BUILDS TRUST

When you make promises they need to be:

- ➡ mutually agreed upon and understood
- ➡ reasonable to achieve
- ➡ explicitly clear
- ➡ related to the betrayal that occurred
- ➡ honored - and not be spontaneously renegotiated when they become uncomfortable or inconvenient

For example, a wife who claimed to be out shopping during the day when in fact she was with another man, might need to check in with her husband more regularly than normal to quell his suspicions and begin to rebuild his trust in her. Or the husband on a business trip, who promises not to drink alcohol while away because it had led to cheating before, needs to follow through with his promise and not call his wife to renegotiate the terms of the promise while on the trip.

KEEP YOUR PROMISES.
Under-promise and Over-deliver.

BE CONSISTENCY IN ACTION.
Follow through with your promises and commitments.

Breaking a promise while trying to rebuild trust can do even more damage than the original transgression because it demonstrates that even when you are on your best behavior, you cannot keep your word.

Follow through on your promises and then talk about it.

When trying to rebuild trust, it is helpful to make a clear, conscious connection for yourself and your partner that the promises you make are actually being kept. Call attention to the fact that what you said you would do, has been done as promised. This reinforces and reminds each of you that your words and actions are honorable and trust worthy.

Keep repeating this -

I LOVE you.
I'm HERE.
WE matter.
YOU are important.
I WANT only you.

HOW CAN I TRUST MYSELF?

How do I make sure I never cheat again?

You are right to feel vulnerable and to question your integrity - you have done wrong and you have the ability to do it again.

First and foremost you must be honest with yourself, and that will allow you to be an honest partner who *communicates* truthfully, clearly, and openly. If you are living in integrity within yourself, it's difficult to live a lie with others.

Start off by refusing to be drawn back in to the affair you left - no contact, no memories, no notes, no songs, nothing that might tempt you or remind you of what you have just left behind - you have to look forward and stay focused on the relationship that truly matters most to you.

You have this new opportunity to make things right, to do better this time, to prove to yourself and your partner that you are someone who has the strength and capability to stay true to your word and your convictions, to be faithful and worthy of trust from the ones that matter the most - the ones who love you.

"Without forgiveness there is no future."

Desmond Tutu

CHAPTER

12

FORGIVENESS
leads to healing

RELATIONSHIP REHAB AND HEALING

WHAT IS FORGIVENESS?

> *"Essentially forgiveness is the willingness to let go of the hurt and no longer suffer. It is a choice to no longer find value in anger, blame, or victimhood. And it is letting go of the desire to hurt another or ourselves because of something that is already in the past. It is the choice to feel love rather than judge or condemn."*
>
> Gerald Jampolsky, M.D.

Forgiving your partner and yourself for what happened in the past, allows you to live and love more freely, generously, and peacefully in the present. To forgive is to give yourself the relief of letting go of all the pain that holds you back from love and loving. Forgiveness is declaring *"I'm not carrying this anymore!"* and instead saying *"yes"* to life again, *"yes"* to love again.

Forgiveness is not for your partner, it's for you.

*Did YOU know? Forgiveness is **not** weakness... Forgiveness is a sign of **strength***

Forgiveness is something you have to decide to do. It's a conscious decision to not throw away your relationship nor the memories, life, or home you've built together. It's the choice to make the future better and set yourself FREE.

The purpose of forgiveness is to release YOU from the past and free you from the imprisonment of your own grudges and grievances. Forgiveness is about allowing yourself to finally cleanse, heal, and let go of the wounds of your betrayal and hurt so that you can live in present time with more peace.

THE TOP 12 REASONS PEOPLE DON'T FORGIVE

1. If I forgive my partner, aren't I sending a message that I'm OK with what they have done?

2. My heart feels frozen, I doubt I'll ever melt. Forgiving will make me feel too vulnerable.

3. My partner really hurt me and did me wrong. Why should I forgive? They deserve my withdrawal, anger, blame and punishment.

4. I don't want to ever get caught unaware again. If I forgive, my partner might do the same thing again.

5. I'll be seen as weak or having no backbone if I forgive. What does that say about me if I just let them off the hook after they cheated?

6. I'd have no self-respect. Only a desperate loser would forgive their partner for something like this.

7. It's too soon to forgive.

8. I like the control. If I forgive, my partner will stop trying so hard. I don't want to lose the control I have.

9. Not forgiving, keeps my guard up, so that I'm aware and protected.

10. I'm so angry that my partner cheated, lied, and betrayed me, I can't ever imagine forgiving them.

11. It's OK to forgive a little at a time, but to never forgive, totally and completely.

12. I would love to let go of the anger and despair I feel but if I do, I could be hurt and betrayed again.

THE TOP 12 REASONS YOU SHOULD FORGIVE

1. Because you and your partner are choosing to stay together, work on your relationship and renew intimacy and closeness.

2. Because your partner is proving themselves to be sincerely remorseful, resolute on rebuilding your relationship, taking responsibility for their actions and trustworthy in their follow through.

3. Because you find no value in withholding love and disconnecting from yourself and your partner using self- pity, faultfinding, judgment, victimization, punishment, and hurt.

4. Because you are ready to count your blessings rather than counting the hurts.

5. Because you choose to make peace of mind, happiness and love your goal.

6. Because you are tired of the suffering and emotional pain that holding onto grudges, grievances, and unforgiving thoughts causes you.

7. Because you choose empowerment over victimhood and to free yourself from the hurtful past to live in the present moment, stronger, wiser, and in control of life's choices and focus.

8. Because you don't see any value in punishing yourself with unhappy, fearful thoughts.

9. Because you recognize that by forgiving you are not agreeing with, absolving, forgetting or condoning your partner's cheating, you are choosing the peace and happiness that comes to you when you forgive.

10. Because by forgiving you can take control of your life back by choosing to restore faith and rebuild trust.

11. Because you recognize that what you think affects how you feel and you no longer want to live held in bondage by the negative emotions that are eating you alive.

12. Because it's time to let go of the anger towards yourself, your partner, and the relationship you had together in the past. This isn't easy, but carrying anger, resentment, grudges, and hostility in your heart is as physically and emotionally draining as carrying large, heavy buckets of water on your shoulders all day. Not being willing to let go of the hurt, or deciding to hold a grudge and not forgive, truly hurts you more than it hurts your partner.

"When you forgive,
you in no way change the past -
but you sure do change the future."
Bernard Meltzer

"To not *forgive* is
a decision to suffer."
Gerald Jampolsky, M.D.

"To *forgive* is to set a prisoner free
and discover that the prisoner was you."
Lewis B. Smedes

SELF-REALIZATIONS

❓ When you invest in blame, judgment, criticism and victimization, what do you receive in return?

❓ Does making your partner feel bad bring any real benefit to you personally?

❓ Or is it actually causing you harm?

❓ Does feeling bad serve anyone?

❓ Why cause yourself continued unnecessary pain?

When you hold on to your grudges, when you refuse to forgive, the only one you are really hurting is yourself.

Did YOU know?

WRITING down your feelings can HELP with the forgiveness process

Be honest with your words, and your thoughts will begin to take shape

Take a moment and think about what it would feel like in your mind, body, and heart if you invested the same time and energy in forgiveness, acceptance, understanding, love and harmony...

YOU can choose to release these grievances and create a miracle.

Listen to the voice of love
NOT *the voice of blame*

"We can look at forgiveness as a journey across an imaginary bridge from a world where we are always recycling our hurt and anger to a place of peace and expanding love."

Gerald Jampolsky, M.D.

Take a moment and actually answer the
questions below - you will be glad you did...

I'm afraid to forgive my partner because....

_____

_____

_____

I want to forgive my partner because....

_____

_____

_____

*How do I feel emotionally, physically, and spiritually, when I
think about the affair?*

_____

_____

_____

*The possible difference it could make in my life if I could let
these feelings and thoughts go is....*

_____

_____

_____

The fears I have in letting go of these feelings are....

_____

_____

_____

If I forgive, what would I give up?

_____

_____

_____

If I forgive, what would I gain?

_____

_____

_____

"IT IS NOT ENOUGH TO KNOW THAT
LOVE AND FORGIVENESS ARE POSSIBLE
WE HAVE TO FIND WAYS TO BRING THEM TO LIFE."

Nelson Mandela

7 STEPS TO FORGIVENESS:

Step 1: ALLOW YOURSELF TO FORGIVE

Verbally, out loud, give yourself permission to forgive. It may not come easily, but it is the best course for you and your partner. No matter what the outcome of your relationship may be; allowing yourself to heal, allows you to move on and beyond.

Step 2: LOOK BEYOND THE NOW

If you are unwilling to see further than the pain and anger, the hurt and confusion, then you will be miserable as long as you let yourself wallow in the past. You must see beyond the pain of today and project a brighter future into the next few weeks and months. See yourself, loving, free, clear, and happy. See yourself forgiving, trusting more, and feeling closer than ever before. You have nothing to lose and peace of mind to gain.

Step 3: CONTROL YOUR EMOTIONS

Remember where resentment, anger and jealousy originate – within you! As much as these feelings might well up inside you, it is imperative that you do not allow these emotions to control or overwhelm you. While your partner had the affair, your challenge is, time and time again, to come back to yourself and see that you are 100% responsible for your emotions. You have to take hold of yourself and think beyond them, take control and choose to change your emotional response from being a victim to being victorious.

Step 4: GIVE UP THE PAST

Going over and over what your partner has done and how they should not have done it is a road to nowhere. And I want you to go somewhere - somewhere good. What happened is what happened. What you choose to do from here will determine the future. So give up the past, stop worrying about what cannot be controlled and get on with what you two can do to make this better.

Step 5: CHOOSE TO FORGIVE

Wanting to forgive is the first step to forgiving. Every time you say 'yes' to focusing on what is good and loveable about your partner, instead of focusing on the pain and heart ache, it strengthens and frees you. Keep making the conscious choice to love and heal. You will be glad you did.

Step 6: FORGIVE IN DOSES

Trying to forgive everything at once is an unrealistic goal - so rather than trying to do too much at once, forgive in doses... Forgive on a minute-by-minute basis, forgive a little at a time and in the end you will have forgiven everything.

Step 7: RISE WITH FORGIVENESS

When you wake up, when the light hits your eyes, decide that you are going to forgive today, for the whole day... You might feel the surge rise up to feel bitter, but if you remember the deal you made with yourself in the morning it will help you move through it.

EMOTIONAL SEX SCENARIO

Although it wasn't always easy, I'm glad I hung in there and did the work necessary to forgive my wife. I came to realize that I didn't want to allow one stupid act to cancel out a lifetime of intimacy, sharing, and commitment. Instead of staying wrapped up in my anger, I chose to focus on the positive things my wife had done - the good mother she was to our children, the supportive friend she had always been to me, the loving companionship she offered. For me, forgiveness was necessary so that my love could breathe again. Our bond and love is stronger and closer than ever. I no longer worry or wonder if my wife will cheat again. With forgiveness, came relief.

Forgiveness comes as **trust** *is built*
Forgiveness is a **happening** *not a step*

FOR THE UNFAITHFUL PARTNER

How do I forgive myself for what I've done to my partner (and family)?

One of the greatest obstacles to forgiving yourself when you feel that you've done wrong, is the burden of shame and sense of guilt that beats you up (once the love chemicals from the affair settle and you are back in your 'right' mind). Racked with guilt, you might be waiting for your partner to forgive you before you forgive yourself.

However, in order to rebuild love, trust, and connection in your relationship, it's not ONLY your partner's forgiveness, but your own that you must seek. While you want your partner's forgiveness, the love, compassion, empathy, understanding and absolution you need must first begin inside of you and INCLUDE YOU. How else can you be open to fully receive it and believe it from your partner?

You must learn to forgive yourself.

---

* NEWS FLASH *

Guilt *and* **self-loathing** DON'T work
and only lead to MORE of the same

What are the blocks to forgiving yourself?

Do you believe that...

➡ feeling bad about your affair, makes you good?

➡ not forgiving yourself, somehow keeps you faithful?

➡ you can stop beating yourself up and still remain account-able for your actions?

Feeling BAD, wrong, and unworthy doesn't lead to good behavior, positive change nor **LOVE**. We attract what we believe. What happens around you is a reflection of what's happening within you. What you see, feel, believe is reflected back with astounding accuracy.

If you believe that your unfaithful actions make you unworthy of your partner's love, then what do you imagine will get reflected back from your partner? More love? I don't think so.

Try... Pain, punishment and emotional purgatory.

Yes, you made a mistake, a **BIG** one.

But, rather than beating yourself up, a healthier choice would be to forgive yourself while accepting responsibility for your own actions. Taking responsibility means that you are willing to look inside and make the necessary changes in your thinking and behavior that led to the infidelity.

It entails actually forgiving yourself and giving yourself permission to do the work necessary to shed the hurt, pain, and anger and allow the healing process to happen.

✔ Write down all the events you wish to seek forgiveness from yourself.

✔ Take responsibility for your actions and choices.

✔ Recognize the hurt you have caused.

✔ Examine the lessons you have learned about yourself.

✔ Take note of which mistakes you made actually contributed to your growth and the growth of your relationship.

✓ Ask yourself, what needs to be healed in order not to repeat the past.

✓ Be prepared to do what is necessary to repair the hurt and pain you caused.

List the ways you have attempted to make amends to yourself, take responsibility, own your choice to cheat, and make amends to yourself and your partner.

_____

_____

_____

_____

_____

_____

_____

_____

In order to rebuild a solid relationship with your partner, you must stand strong and resolute in **LOVE**.

Forgiveness is a vital ingredient in restoring trust, healing yourself and being available to love your partner.

When you forgive yourself, you free up space for more of what you do want in life.

LOVE *begins* inside **YOU.**

"Wipe your emotional slate clean.

Erase the accounts of your past with a bold tongue,

a resolute mind, and a courageous heart."

David Roppo

"I accept and love you as you are.
You can be you.
I can be me."

ACCEPTANCE CONTRACT *by Virginia Satir*

CHAPTER

13

HAVING A GREAT RELATIONSHIP

Rebuilding the Romance.
Strengthening the LOVE

RELATIONSHIP REHAB AND HEALING

Romance makes us feel good because it's all about cherishing, celebrating, and expressing the love that is.

Loving again involves seeing each other with innocent eyes, accepting each other's unique individuality, enjoying being together, and caring for each other's well being.

Your **car** needs gasoline
& your **body** needs food
your **intimate relationship** NEEDS
romantic attention and energy to keep it
thriving and running well

Romance is vital to keeping your relationship alive because it is the language of love that you speak to each other.

When we first fall in love, romance is easy. Surging hormones and pleasure boosting dopamine, create the neurochemical cocktail driving us to bond and mate. We enter what I call "The Romantic State of Mind".

Unfortunately this euphoria doesn't last. The focused ATTENTION, APPRECIATION and AFFECTION that was so easy and natural to give each other while courting, begins to get diverted or diluted by other things. If left unchecked for too long, couples begin to drift apart and emotionally disconnect.

That's when people begin to look outside their relationship to get their emotional and physical needs met. Your relationship thrives and survives on intimate contact and connection.

Romance is the food of love.
Let's face it, everybody wants to hear and know that he or she is loved.

SPEAK THE LANGUAGE OF LOVE YOUR PARTNER UNDERSTANDS

The important thing is to know your partner's language, because what may FEEL loving to you may not FEEL loving to your partner. And vice versa.

Let me tell you about Jack, whose love language is words. Jack continually told his wife Susan how much he loved her, sending her texts, leaving love notes in drawers, and complimenting her often. But Susan continually questioned Jack's love and complained that she never really believed him because his actions didn't match his words. That's one of the things that led Jack to his cyber-emotional affair with Becky whose love language was also through words. What Jack never understood is that Susan felt most loved during the times Jack wanted to spend time with her. Whether it be snuggling on the couch, shopping at Home Depot, or taking a long walk after dinner. While Susan liked hearing that she was loved, she always felt Jack's words were a cover up and untrue because he never seemed to want to spend time with her. Susan's love language is spoken and heard through action, not words. Now that Jack knows Susan's language, he speaks LOVE to her in the language that matters most to her. While expressing LOVE feels good in all the love dialects, when you speak in the particular language of your partner's heart and psyche, it communicates LOVE on the deepest of levels.

As Dr. Gary Chapman points out in his book, *The Five Love Languages*, it is imperative to speak in your partner's LOVE LANGUAGE.

No matter how long you've been together, do you REALLY know what makes your partner feel most loved by you?

Have you ever asked?

Is it when you use WORDS to tell your partner how much you love them?

i.e. praising in front of others, talking sweetly, writing love notes, talking through the issues, being open about your thoughts and feelings, listening and understanding, reading love poems to each other, sending love texts throughout the day, expressing your gratitude.

Is it when you SHOW your love with loving actions?

i.e. jumping in and helping around the house without being asked, going grocery shopping together, displaying kindness and thoughtfulness, showing respect, pampering, having the candles lit and dinner on the table when he comes home, giving space and time when she needs it, bringing them a latte in bed in the morning, taking care when sick, standing up and taking responsibility for your actions.

Is it spending time doing things TOGETHER?

i.e. being playful together, having the same hobby or interest, taking a walk after dinner, holding each other on the couch watching TV, a romantic picnic at the beach, going to sporting events, working together on a project and solving problems, showing that you WANT to be together.

Is it through TOUCH and expressing physical affection?

i.e. is it through outward signs of affection, kissing your partner the way they want to be kissed, touching with tenderness, giving a foot rub for no reason, reaching to hold hands, wearing sensual clothing when coming to bed.

Is it showing up with THOUGHTful gifts and surprises?

i.e. buying little things, giving unconditional gifts of love, putting thought into the presents you give, flowers for no reason, planning a romantic date and keeping the details a surprise.

When you speak in the LOVE LANGUAGE of your partner's heart

romance and intimacy flourish

I'm often asked by couples, "What does it take to jump start our stagnated relationship and restore the romantic, passionate feelings that first brought us together?"

For over a decade, my answer has been the same:

"Give each other the 3 A's."

Giving and receiving positive **ATTENTION, APPRECIATION** and **AFFECTION** fuels the fire of your romantic life, strengthens the core connection your relationship needs to thrive, and helps maintain the balance between intimacy and the demands of everyday life.

Knowing that you are loved, valued, known and accepted is fundamental to having a better life and a better love.

Daily exchanges of the **3 A's** cultivate closeness, emotional safety, and more loving behavior that translates into having a great relationship.

"The love we give away is the only love we keep."

Elbert Hubbard

Let me ask you **3** simple questions:

On a *daily* basis how much positive and loving...

Attention - **do you give and receive from your partner?**

Appreciation - **do you give and receive from your partner?**

Affection - **do you give and receive from your partner?**

ATTENTION: Spending quality time together, communicating, sharing, building your friendship, and having fun.

APPRECIATION: Being generous with praise, gratitude and acknowledgement. Noticing and commenting on the good stuff - big and small - sharing your admiration often. Seeing each other anew with fresh eyes every day.

AFFECTION: Staying in contact. Embracing regularly. Kissing often. Giving comfort. Smiling frequently. Reaching over and touching each other whenever possible.

Give each other healthy portions of the 3A's EVERYDAY

"I know that what is for me... knows me... claims me...

and rushes to me."

Ernest Holmes

ATTENTION

Pay Attention. Everyday.

HOW YOU BEHAVE BECOMES **YOU**

"Love at first sight is easy to understand; it's when two people have been looking at each other for a lifetime that it becomes a miracle."

Amy Bloom

Where are you putting your ATTENTION?

- ❓ How do you share your time together?

- ❓ What pulls your attention more, your love or your complaints?

- ❓ How much time is spent making love with your partner (not just sexually)?

- ❓ What daily attention do you give to romance and love in your relationship?

You FEEL What You FOCUS On
Thoughts lead to feelings which lead to behavior.

When you are focused on what is missing and wrong, those things begin to dominate your perceptions. This poisons the relationship and inevitably causes couples to drift apart. The antidote is to stop dwelling on the negative and to celebrate the positive.

Start with the love that IS. Direct your focus on the good things that are working, what you love and admire in each other, and the fun things that bring joy.

When you direct your attention to loving your partner it WILL make your relationship more passionate and fun.

Do at least THREE things
that will ENHANCE your union **EVERY DAY**

There are many ways to say and to show, I LOVE YOU.

Romance is **saying** *"I love you,"* **showing** *"I love you,"* **feeling** *"I love you."*

If you do this a minimum of 3 times a day, you will notice a difference, you will feel closer to each other, and your bond will be stronger for it.

SPEAK YOUR PARTNER'S **LOVE LANGUAGE**
FLUENTLY AND OFTEN

Let's face it, we all want to hear and know that we are loved. As I discussed earlier, it's important to regularly speak and show your partner (in their love language) that you love them through your actions and your words. Here are a few ideas to get the LOVE-ball rolling.

- ♥ Put love notes in surprise places...on your partner's pillow, briefcase or in the book they're reading.

- ♥ Create a clandestine signal that says 'I Love You' that only the two of you know and then send it often.

- ♥ Say "I love you" at least three times a day, in different ways, at different times.

♥ Start the foreplay early - call during the day and leave a message on your partner's cell phone of what you'd like to do to him or have her do to you.

♥ Before rushing out the door in a frenzy, get up earlier with your partner, have breakfast in bed, read an inspirational passage aloud, hold each other, go for a walk, give each other a massage, take a shower together.

♥ Walk your partner to the door when leaving and seal it with a kiss. Kisses are the food of love. A loving embrace of the lips.

It's the little things *we say or do that mean a lot.*

Spend more time, positive, quality time, just together...enjoying. Time when you're not talking about the affair. Doing new things together can be a fun way to connect and keep things interesting. It can be as simple as trying a new restaurant or going on a day trip to a place you've never been before. Use this time as an opportunity to rediscover your partner anew, because in seeing with the eyes of discovery and curiosity, you can hopefully notice something new and interesting that you like and want to learn more about.

The moment we give close attention to anything, even a blade of grass it becomes a mysterious, awesome, indescribably magnificent world in itself. Give your partner this curious attention.

This attitude of interested curiosity brings romance back. Yes, romance — at first the last thing the betrayed partner may want to do, especially right after discovering there's been an affair in the midst, is to get close. But, slowly by approaching each other, communicating with absolute honesty, (the truth does set you free), spending more quality, positive time together, starting to go out on dates together, expressing love through action, building trust and starting to see each other anew, romance may blossom like a well watered rose in summer.

*Spend **quality time together** on a regular basis -*

*That is a form of **ATTENTION***

You don't have to make BIG plans, invest a lot of time or make GRAND romantic gestures to stir your partner's heart.

That is what our anniversary or Valentine's Day is set up to do.

While extraordinary gestures certainly have their place, it's the daily small things that count. It's the ways you show, say, and celebrate *"I love you. We're in love! This is great!"* And mean it. Come on, bring some joy into it.

It's critical for your relationship, to **MAKE THE TIME** to be TOGETHER.

Find something that you enjoy doing together, whether it is a shared hobby, dance class, daily walk, or sitting over a cup of coffee in the morning. Even during busy and stressful times, a few minutes of really sharing and connecting can help keep bonds strong. And, just like in the beginning, try something new together.

Doing new things together can be a fun way to connect and keep things interesting. It can be as simple as trying a new restaurant or going on a day trip to a place you've never been before.

APPRECIATION

Recognize, Honor and Praise.

"Feeling grateful or appreciative of someone or something in your life actually attracts more of the things that you appreciate and value into your life."

Christiane Northrup

Do This Appreciation Check In:

- ❓ Do you assume your partner knows how you **feel**?

- ❓ How does your partner know that he/she is **valued** by you?

- ❓ How **cherished** and appreciated do you feel in your relationship?

- ❓ Do you express your appreciation and gratitude to each other out loud?

In essence, appreciation involves looking for what is good versus what is bad. Let your partner know **OUT LOUD** when you are thinking **GOOD** things about them. It's just being a little more generous with your praise, acknowledgement and gratitude. And it's so easy to do!

It's as simple as giving your partner a couple of compliments a day, a wink of recognition, a hug of thanks. It almost doesn't matter what you focus on with your appreciation:

"Wow, you look beautiful!"

"I am so lucky I married you."

"Thank you for sweeping the floor, it looks great."

It's the recognition that you are appreciating and seeing how important your partner is to the mainstay of your relationship, and in your life. That sort of seeing, acknowledging, and expression of positive regard communicates so much more than the words convey.

The underlying core message you are sending is:

"I value you."

"You are important to me."

"What you're doing is important for us."

"Because of you, my life is so much better."

Your partner naturally feels more accepted, loved, and valued. This feeds romance more deliciously than a great dinner out on the town. Make your partner feel good about themselves every day.

Don't assume that they know. SAY IT, and say it in words and show it in your actions, such as hugging and loving and saying thank you.

*Share **5** things you are grateful for **about each other and the relationship...***

each and **every day**

Dr. Leo Buscaglia in his book, *'Living, Loving and Learning,'* describes qualities of a loving relationship that truly touches my heart and I'd love to share with you:

> *"Starting each day I shall remember to communicate my joy as well as my despair, so that we can know each other better. Starting each day, I shall remind myself to really listen to you and to try to hear your point of view, and discover the least-threatening way of giving you mine, remembering that we're both growing and changing in a hundred different ways. Starting each day, I shall try to be more aware of the beautiful things in our world...and I'll share those these things with you. Starting each day, I shall remind myself to reach out and touch you, gently, with my words, my eyes, and my fingers because I don't want to miss feeling you. Starting each day I shall dedicate myself again to the process of being a lover, and then see what happens."*

AFFECTION

Keep in touch. Embrace often.

"Happy marriages begin when we marry the ones we love, and they blossom when we love the ones we marry."

Tom Mullen

Often, we think affection is sex, or a strategy for having sex. And, that's certainly one way to communicate your love. But AFFECTION is touching heart to heart, not just body to body. It's your words and open hearted gestures that say I love you and express closeness. It's stroking each other as you walk by. It's sending a kiss across the room. It's making eye contact and really seeing each other. It's hugging and holding each other. As a matter of fact, being affectionate is GOOD for your health and well being. Doctors have found that touching and being touched helps us to thrive. Studies have shown that affectionate touch actually boosts the body's levels of oxytocin, a hormone that influences bonding and attachment. It takes little time to open your arms to one another and has huge benefits. Giving lots of warm hugs to your partner is a great way to strengthen your ability to give and receive affection. AFFECTION is showing your LOVE IN ACTION using touch, contact, and staying in touch.

Loving eye contact is a powerful tool for bonding and enhancing intimacy. Being truly seen and taken in is an aphrodisiac. Hold hands, take 3 deep breaths and smile into each other's eyes. If feelings come up, let them. You'll be surprised how profound and arousing deeply looking into each other's eyes can be for both of you.

Touch is a fundamental part of human existence.

Try to really focus on the mood your partner is in - as much as touch is affection in action, it can sometimes be irritation in action if it is done too forcefully or at an inappropriate time. Be sensitive to your partner's emotions and to the timing and strength of your touch.

How do you like to be touched? **Tell your partner**

"The biggest blessing in life is finding that one special person that somehow knows how to touch you at the deepest part of your soul. No matter what is circling around you... this makes you feel like everything is going to be ok."

Bryan Lund

Do you have **20** *seconds?*

Then you have time for romance!

Did
YOU know?

Affectionate touch boosts the body's feel good hormones

•••

Holding hands relieves stress

7 FUN WAYS TO AFFECTIONATELY EXPLORE, TOUCH, STROKE AND STOKE PASSION'S FLAMES

You can 'make love' all day long.

Here are 7 easy ways:

1. Give your partner a 20 second kiss when they walk in the door or are leaving for the day.

2. Hold hands, take 3 deep breaths, and smile into each other's eyes - take a moment to feel your whole body as it is - profound moments can happen when you look deeply into each other's eyes.

3. Make a game of kissing. Kissing at commercial breaks. Kissing at red lights. Kissing when you spot a white Lexus.

4. Whispering changes our state of mind. Whisper sweet and adoring things into your partner's ear.

5. Touch each other without using your hands. You can touch with any part of your body, your hair, your feet, your arms. There are parts of your body that are seldom touched that are especially sensitive. See if you can find these parts on your partner's body - and on your own.

6. Brush against your partner in a sexually seductive way. Be playful with your touch. Give him a seductive smile. Put your arms around her. Kiss the back of his neck. Give her a slight caress whenever you pass by.   Blow a kiss to each other across the room.

7. Give each other a head massage.

A kiss can lift the moment from ordinary
to intimately extraordinary

"Then I did the simplest thing in the world. I leaned down... and kissed him. And the world cracked open."

Agnes de Mille

Kissing is critical to bonding and making love. It's a great way to express affection, is one of the most intimate and loving acts two people can do together, and it communicates so much.

Each kiss can wordlessly say,

"Welcome home."

"I cherish you."

"I'm yours."

"I'm sorry."

"I'm here for you."

Kissing feels *good*. There are so many nerve endings in your lips that connect to the feel g*ood* portion of your brain. When you start kissing, it releases oxytocin through your body, which is the bonding hormone, and brings you closer.

Kiss your partner deeply, deliberately, and dearly OFTEN.

"Her kisses left something to be desired...

the rest of her."

Author Unknown

RECOVERING SEXUAL DESIRE AFTER AN AFFAIR

Emotional Sex Scenario

"To be honest the first time we made love after I found out about the affair was the most passionate and pleasurable lovemaking that we've experience in years. At first I was afraid to touch him or have any sexual contact. But, we've been growing emotionally closer, I'm feeling safer and our kissing has been arousing me to say the least. What I didn't expect was all the mixed up emotions I had. I cried for hours after because all I could imagine was him holding and doing the same things to her. I feel so open, vulnerable and confused. Is it weird to still desire my husband after he had an affair or is it that I just desperately want to feel he still loves and wants me? I am amazed that the sex is better now than ever."

When is the best time to resume physical sex again?

The answer: When you're both ready.

It all starts OUTSIDE the BEDROOM. Often the closer you get emotionally, the more you build trust, and are on the road to happiness, the more ready you'll be.

If you both enjoy sex, and you both want it, anytime is the right time. Often for women, sexual desire flows with feeling safe and good about yourself.

Maintaining open communication, regaining emotional intimacy, spending relaxing and fun time together, and filling your relationship with the **3 A's** tend to light the fire of libidos and sex drives.

COMMUNICATE THROUGH *EVERY* STAGE OF **RECONNECTION**

- ◉ Don't RUSH IT.

- ◉ Don't do it because you FEEL PRESSURED.

- ◉ Make Sure Your SELF ESTEEM Is In The Right Place

WHEN THE TIME IS RIGHT, YOU WILL KNOW.

Ultimately, we all want to be in a great relationship, but no relationship is great just *because*. We have to work at it.

Give each other the **3 A's** - **ATTENTION, APPRECIATION** and **AFFECTION** - on a day-to-day basis. This will set up a strong foundation for your relationship.

Romance comes easily when you are mindful of the **3 A's** - in fact, romance is inherent in the **3 A's** and romance flourishes because of the **3 A's** - you find yourselves in a circular motion of giving and receiving love, appreciation, and affection which improves your relationship daily and makes love feel alive.

When you are present, aware, and attentive, you become sensitive and attuned to each other's needs and desires. Needs are more easily fulfilled when heard and responded to without stress. This builds safety and trust.

You love your partner, you are committed to them, you show them that love by your words and actions, by being the person you want to be and by being the person they want to be with.

Allow your relationship to be flexible and enjoyable by realizing that love is a work of art that should never be completed, it should be constantly nurtured and admired, enjoyed and respected - just like your partner.

CHAPTER

14

ROADMAP FOR CHANGE

Create a Partnership Vision

RELATIONSHIP REHAB AND HEALING

You obviously love your partner and he or she loves you, which is why you have decided to forgive and move on.

But, if you do not know where you are going, how can you expect to get there? By now, both of you probably recognize that you don't want to RETURN to the way it WAS.

The OLD ways of communicating, communing, and caring did NOT work.

To avoid getting pulled back into the past, set your mind and heart on creating a new, shared **RELATIONSHIP VISION** of what being together means to each of you.

Creating a **RELATIONSHIP VISION** is an important part of *affair-proofing* your relationship.

Writing a CO-CREATED vision statement allows you and your partner to hold hands and together consciously determine the course of your relationship as you envision the partnership that you would like to live in.

Think of this RELATIONSHIP VISION as a ROADMAP...

... a **ROADMAP** to use on your journey of healing, mending and building a heart-healthy love connection together. This **ROADMAP** gives your partnership a mutual understanding of the direction, structure, and intimacy you each want in your relationship.

CO-CREATING a new, conscious *WE* **ROADMAP** of your evolving hopes, desires, and expectations will help your relationship to repair and move on with better understanding.

This **ROADMAP** inspires trust because you both KNOW that you are on the same page. It helps you focus on a new VISION and a clear **direction** of what you mutually want and agree to.

When we enter a committed relationship, we usually bring a suitcase full of hopes, dreams, assumptions, and expectations that have evolved since childhood about what love, relationship, and commitment means to us.

Some of these expectations which are conscious are usually shared and communicated - *"I want children." "I expect monogamy." "I believe a happy couple tells each other everything."*

We also, often unknowingly, bring expectations and distorted perspectives about love from our childhood and prior romantic experiences that are hidden underground, denied, or unknown to us and thus, unspoken. These are the expectations that lead to conflict, disappointment, disillusionment, and acting out later on. The more you bring these to light and talk about them, the less they'll secretly dictate your relationship patterns and reactions.

release and replace
the old painful patterns *and* disappointment triggers

A successful relationship vision should be aligned with each of your core values and relationship needs - it should be infused with sources that give each of you happiness and a sense of well-being.

Wouldn't a relationship that honors your personal needs and fulfills your relationship needs be wonderful? Building a co-created relationship vision together is a great way to start consciously creating the partnership you both REALLY want to have.

HOW TO BUILD A ROADMAP FOR YOUR RELATIONSHIP

Find a quiet time when the two of you will be free from distractions to design and create your vision.

Hold hands and play together.

Let yourself DREAM and have fun, discussing, jotting down and sharing the things that you have always wanted for yourself and your relationship.

Then, work as a team, work on your VISION and on the goals that honor and recognize your needs, wants and desires.

Phrase everything in the positive. Some examples might be:

"We kiss at every red light."

"We settle our differences calmly."

"We play golf together every Saturday."

"We sit down and talk to each other daily."

"We laugh a lot together and are playfully affectionate."

Your VISION will manifest into life as you set forth and put your specific goals into place.

Grab a pen, grab each other's hands, sit down and focus on where you are going and on the RELATIONSHIP you want to have with each other.

First **DREAM**, then **DISCUSS**, then **ACT**

Become the **architect of your future**
                instead of a victim of the past

A VISION, like your RELATIONSHIP is not carved in stone and will grow and change as you and your partner listen, learn, and deepen your LOVE.

You have NOTHING TO LOSE
             AND EVERYTHING TO GAIN

SOME IDEAS FOR YOUR RELATIONSHIP VISION ROADMAP

What is great and what needs improvement in the following areas?

- Being on the SAME team.
- How you raise your children.
- How you spend/save money.
- Appreciation, respect and care.
- Sharing activities - fun and play.
- Physical sexuality and sensuality.
- Faithfulness, loyalty and honesty.
- Open communication and sharing.
- Supporting - having each other's back.
- Personal career goals and desired changes.
- Honoring, respecting and cherishing each other.
- Together time - amount of time spent together.
- Autonomy and space - amount of time needed apart.
- Ability to respect differing opinions and move forward.
- How love, care, and affection are shown and expressed.
- Ways you or your partner handle frustrations, anger or hurts.
- Ability to take responsibility, own your mistakes and say I'm sorry.
- Time spent with in-laws, parents, siblings and other family members.
- Skills or hobbies that you would like to develop, share or have supported.
- Feeling safe and accepted to be transparent, authentic and fully share who you are.

adapted from Getting the Love You Want: A Guide for Couples
by Harville Hendrix Ph.D

Creating this RELATIONSHIP VISION ROADMAP together helps to guide you along the way and especially to *affair-proof* your relationship by taking control of your own relationship story's happy ending.

Creating the VISION is one half of a process. The next part is to LIVE the vision

---

After you create your roadmap, it is time to put it into action and bring your relationship vision to **life**.

Type it up on nice paper using an easy to read font, and post it on the refrigerator, your bathroom mirror or someplace you will easily see it each day. Once a week, sit down together read your vision out loud and choose one action that you both will commit to doing for seven days.

Example: *"We sit down and talk every day."*

One action step might be to commit to choosing a place to talk and be together, uninterrupted for 15 minutes, every night.

And then do it for seven days in a row. After seven days, take a new one from the list and add it to your routine.

Visioning is seeing with the heart. It is seeing possibilities. It is seeing what could be. Vision is powerful, and a shared vision is even more so.

"A vision is not just a picture of what could be; it is an appeal to our better selves, a call to become something more."

Rosabeth Moss Kanter

CHAPTER

15

A HEALTHY, HEART-HAPPY PARTNERSHIP

Exercising Your Relationship Muscle

RELATIONSHIP REHAB AND HEALING

7 WAYS TO VACCINATE YOUR RELATIONSHIP

against the Threat of Cyber, Emotional and Physical **INFIDELITY**

1. Stay alert for temptations and choose friends wisely.

Know your vulnerable, dangerous places and stay away from them. Making friends on Facebook, at work, or reconnecting with an ex can be very exciting, especially when this is a person who shares the same interests, lifestyle, or past with you. However, these 'friends' can become attractive when your relationship is vulnerable. Do not 'friend' anyone that your partner would disapprove of. If someone poses ANY threat to your relationship, de-friend the person!

2. Keep your personal life and relationship matters PERSONAL.

A lot of emotional bonding occurs when people start confiding, complaining, colluding, and revealing. That's when hearts open, guards are let down, boundaries are crossed, and things just evolve. You can still grow a friendship without crossing the line of respect or privacy with your partner. If you need to talk about your emotional issues, talk to your partner, a friend who IS on the partnership side of the fence, or a professional.

3. Don't even consider flirting.

That's how affairs start. You know the difference between innocent friendship and flirting. Put yourself in your partner's place. How would you feel if your partner was doing what you are doing? Love is like a drug. You can be drawn to an affair as to a drug. And once you are past a certain point of emotional connection, it is very hard to go into reverse. Avoid being alone with and/or emotionally close to someone to whom you are emotionally or sexually attracted. Flirting is a sign of attraction.

4. Admit when you are attracted.

If you feel yourself drawn to someone else, admit this to yourself and to your partner, right away. This helps to avoid acting on it. Honesty (the antidote to secrecy and developing special intimacy with another) keeps the relationship from becoming an affair because it's now out in the open, and consciously up for viewing and owning.

5. Remember CHEATING starts with CHATTING.

Especially in cyber space. Beware of the lure of the Internet. An emotional or cyber affair develops quickly, in just a few hours, days, or weeks online, where it might take months or years at the office. There is safety, anonymity, and mystery behind the computer screen that is alluring and addictive. Discuss with your partner which online 'friends' are appropriate and which are inappropriate, and how much personal information is okay to share. Be clear about who (e.g. the ex) and what kind of communication (e.g. sexual banter) is off-limits.

6. Talk in WE language.

Make **WE** a priority. Substitute single words in your vocabulary with partnership words. Single words are *"mine, me, my, I."* Partnership words are *"our, we, us."* Affairs happen when you remain uncoupled in your thoughts, feelings, and actions. Speak often and out loud using **WE** language. *"**WE** are in a committed, monogamous relationship,"* *"**WE** are going out of town this weekend,"* *"**WE** are in this together."*

7. Make sure your social network and friends support your monogamy.

Who are you hanging out with, how often, and where? Think twice about who you're regularly seeing for lunch or having drinks with after work. Drugs and alcohol lower your guard. Surround yourself with happily committed friends who don't believe in fooling around.

An easy way to self-administer the seven affair-proof vaccinations is to simply remember: *Avoid any behavior or 'friendship' that might cause you to put your relationship at risk.*

Stay away from situations that give rise to opportunities that promote infidelity. You now KNOW the signs, the breeding grounds and your vulnerabilities.

Trust your gut feeling and if thoughts of cheating cross your mind, run in the OPPOSITE direction AWAY from that person and TO your partner.

Feeling flirtatious and attracted to another is a BIG RED FLAG that it's time to connect, communicate and infuse your relationship with the 3 A's quickly. Return your focus to building and maintaining a strong, loyal bond of faithfulness with yourself and your partner that you will not break at any cost.

Put your attention to making your relationship strong — grow your emotional intimacy and friendship with your partner.

INTIMACY'S RESCUE KIT

LOVE BOOSTERS & BOLSTERS

Become better friends than before

The best relationship is based on friendship & positive regard.

What makes a relationship work is surprisingly simple. Happy couples have let their positive feelings override their negative ones. They understand, honor, and respect each other. They have an abiding regard for each other's well being and best interest at heart. They know each other deeply and enjoy being together. They do little things each day to stay connected and show each other they care. In short, they are friends. Best Friends.

If you want a friend
be a friend

Friendship is at the core of a strong partnership.

If you want to strengthen your relationship, give attention to building your friendship.

Respecting one another, opening up and telling each other everything — listening, really listening — being real, playing and having fun together cultivates trust, forgiveness, and faithfulness.

According to author and relationship researcher John Gottman, "Friendship between couples means they 'know each other intimately' and are well versed in each other's likes, dislikes, personality quirks, hopes and dreams."

When the friendship is strong, you are more likely to not only love your partner but LIKE him or her too. When your partner IS your best friend, you are less likely to form a secret, intimate, or sexually energized friendship with someone else.

Invest in strengthening the foundation

The foundation of any strong relationship is built on trust, respect, good communication, and friendship. Attend to the little things that build love and show friendship like offering support, being affectionate, spending time together, giving gifts, saying *"I love you"* through actions and words, and standing resolute and strong when storms occur.

Acknowledge the positives and express gratitude

Keep the romance flowing and glowing

Go on dates, get romantic, get close, enjoy each other. Apply the 3 A's often and abundantly. Truly loving couples know that while grand gestures are exciting and sensational for a while, love only grows strong and flourishes in the consistent, steady stream of daily contact, loving attention, consideration, and feeling truly valued.

Set aside time and create an oasis for intimacy in your busy life and guard it as sacred.

---

*Your **mind** is your biggest sexual organ*
What you tell yourself
greatly impacts your level of desire

Create time to be intimate and change your mantra from *"I'm too tired, busy, angry"*... into... *"I'm ready to be pleasured, renewed, and restored."*

Make daily love deposits into your relationship account. A relationship is what two people put into it. Do little things every day to stay connected and show you care about each other. Think of your relationship as a savings account. Keep a healthy balance sheet.

For every one negative thing you do, add 5 positive things. To generate a healthy LOVE return, balance your relationship heavily on the positive side. Each deposit is an appreciation statement, a kind act of thoughtfulness, an expression of love. Notice the kind and generous things your partner does and express gratitude for them. You build up a lot of emotional equity with tenderness, respect and kindness. Focus your attention on your positive feelings about each other, not the negative ones.

---

* Memo to Self:
Make my partner feel good about themselves
every day

Communicate on a daily basis with each other. Talk about practical issues, plans, goals, personal feelings, topics that interest you, problems you are facing and the gratitude you feel.

The little things you talk about are as **important** as the bigger issues

Often your partner doesn't need your advice, they only want you to hear them, hold them, and listen. True romance stems from intimacy and if you're not taking time to talk, listen, and support one another, you will not have much romance.

Don't let irritations build up. Apply the healthy conflict skills you learned in this book. Remember to hold hands as you deal with the storms and conflicts that inevitably arise. Instead of choosing conflict, consider cooperation and collaboration. Cultivate the pause. Take a breather. CALM down. Recognize the pattern and get off the game board. Have a willingness to understand and see your partner's perspective. Put your judgments in the trash. Know that underneath the reactivity is love. Find the love. Search for the love. Make your LOVE VISION stronger than your fear. Use your energy to build a bridge, not a wall. Love your relationship forward. Even when you're not feeling it in the moment.

Change the formula:
*complain **LESS**... make love **MORE***

Stay honest with your partner. Honesty is the trump card for preventing affairs. Deceit and love cannot co-exist. Tell each other everything. OPEN UP, it will bring you CLOSER. Dishonesty, deception, and secrecy cause affairs to flourish. Value the intimacy of your partnership. Reveal as much of yourself to one another as possible. Be real.

Be HONEST with yourself.
And with your partner

Be reliable. Be accepting. Be a safe harbor. Stand resolute when the storms hit. Let your partner know that they are loved and accepted despite differences or problems. Reinforce that you are on the same team and in this together.

Remember: a ME problem is a WE problem

When problems and differences arise, stand strong and say, *"I am here." "I hear you." "YOU are important." "I accept you." "We matter" "I'm not going anywhere." "I'll protect you." "We're in this together." "Our team is strong."*

Be kind, thoughtful, show respect and support each other. Couples that have great relationships have mutual respect and understanding of each other, even when discussing their differences.

Be your partner's chief defender
- NOT their prosecutor

Showing respect means understanding and leaving room for each other's individual needs for space, love, closeness, authenticity, and personal growth.

Remember:
hold hands as you deal with the storms and conflicts

Frequently take your pulse and monitor the relationship heart beat. When something is missing, like sharing, communicating, feeling close, jump on it right away and fix it.

Stay on top of your needs. Are they being expressed and met?

Learn positive ways to deal with stress in your life. Start by noticing when you are out of whack. A good rule of thumb is *pause before you act.* It's important to develop the resiliency to hold up under pressure and meet challenges head-on rather than turning to outside sources such as affairs to get relief. Take charge of your own thoughts, emotions, schedule, and the way YOU deal with problems. Find out what you need to do to relax. Exercise? Meditate? Deep Breathing? Making Love? Do what is necessary to balance your life so that there is time for work, fun, relaxation and lots of LOVE.

Read your RELATIONSHIP VISION out loud. Follow the ROADMAP you have co-created. Choose a new goal weekly. Follow through daily. As you hold hands and bring your shared vision to life, together you become directors of your relationship's journey and writers of your love story's happy ending.

When it comes to relationships

it is not about the destination,

it is about the journey

TURN THE LIGHT OF YOUR HEART BACK ON

When we create an intimate connection with another, the love we share shines through our heart, and the magic we experience comes from our heart.

Sometimes we allow the light of our hearts to fade, and when this happens we open up our heart to outside influences that may cause us to seek the light elsewhere.

But the light is right there, within us - readily available to shine, ready to offer hope, happiness and help to the one who truly deserves it.

If we can re-ignite the passion we feel in our hearts, if we can learn to love generously, then we manifest everything in the world that is good, right and pure.

I urge you to TURN THE LIGHT OF YOUR HEART BACK ON and to enjoy one another once again with renewed energy, with open hearts, with enlightened minds and above all with LOVE.

> *"Where we LOVE is home —*
> *home that our feet may leave,*
> *but not our hearts."*
>
> Oliver Wendell Holmes, Sr.

LIVING IN LOVE

THE ULTIMATE PARTNERSHIP

"I don't pretend to know what love is for everyone, but I can tell you what it is for me; love is knowing all about someone, and still wanting to be with them more than any other person, love is trusting them enough to tell them everything about yourself, including the things you might be ashamed of, love is feeling comfortable and safe with someone, but still getting weak knees when they walk into a room and smile at you."

Unknown

Everyone agrees that love is wonderful, except when it's terrible.

I hope that you will not leave your vision of true love buried in the disappointment of past mistakes - instead, might I suggest that you take that vision of being in a happy, healthy and loving relationship and re-create it from the inside-out and from the outside-in.

For a relationship to succeed, it takes more than an initial spark of attraction, in fact it takes more than love or even commitment — it requires partnership. The path from being in a relationship to having a great partnership is a process.

Like learning to dance together, partners need to practice partnership skills in order to become good at them.

A successful partnership thrives when you nurture it, when you stay curious, eager, attentive, and awake; when you offer daily doses of the **3 A's**, and when you live with honest communication showing up present and grateful, with your arms and heart open wide.

One thing I can tell you is that the couples who have held hands and weathered the storm of **EMOTIONAL SEX** are far stronger, happier and more in love than they ever were before the infidelity occurred. Yes, the rebuilding process took them time, hard work and dedication because it is not easy to open your heart to love and trust again, once betrayed. But you can and will have an amazing relationship on the other end of this journey if you follow the suggestions in this book.

All in all, a formidable and successful relationship is about becoming a team, holding each other's hand, and saying in words, actions and deeds...

I LOVE you.
I'm HERE.
WE matter.
YOU are important.
I WANT only you.

From everything I have seen, heard, and experienced, the more we LIVE IN LOVE and make each other's arms our heart's true home, the easier it becomes to be faithful, accepting and grateful. The more grateful we feel, the more love will live within us and around us.

I am honored to have been your guide on this journey. I wish you the very best of LOVE and a relationship filled with mutual respect, fun, camaraderie and joy that gives you a lifetime of pleasure and happiness.

Straight from MY heart to yours.

REFERENCES AND RECOMMENDED READING

Want to read more?

Here are some great books on related topics that I highly recommend.

Abrahms, Janice & Michael Spring. *After the Affair: Healing the Pain and Rebuilding Trust When a Partner Has Been Unfaithful.* New York: Perennial (1996)

Amen, Daniel. *The Brain in Love: 12 Lessons to Enhance Your Love Life.* New York: Three Rivers Press (2009)

Amen, Daniel. *Change Your Brain, Change Your Life: The Breakthrough Program for Conquering Anxiety, Depression, Obsessiveness, Anger, and Impulsiveness.* New York: Three Rivers Press (1999)

Branden, Nathaniel. *The Psychology of Romantic Love: Romantic Love in an Anti-Romantic Age.* Tarcher (2008)

Buscaglia, Leo. *Living, Loving and Learning.* New York: Ballantine Books (1985)

Buscaglia, Leo. *Born for Love: Reflections on Loving.* New York: Fawcett Columbine (1994)

Carter, Steven and Julia Sokol. *He's Scared, She's Scared: Understanding the Hidden Fears That Sabotage Your Relationships.* New York: Dell (1993)

Carter, Steven. *This is How Love Works: 9 Essential Secrets You Need to Know.* New York: M. Evans and Co. (2001)

Chapman, Gary. The *Five Love Languages: How to Express Heartfelt Commitment to Your Mate.* Chicago: Northfield Publishing (2004)

De Angelis, Barbara. *How to Make Love All the Time: Make Love Last a Lifetime.* New York: Dell (1991)

De Angelis, Barbara. *How Did I Get Here?: Finding Your Way to Renewed Hope and Happiness When Life and Love Take Unexpected Turns.* St. Martin's Griffin (2006)

Deida, David. *Intimate Communion: Awakening Your Sexual Essence.* Dearfield Beach: Health Communications, Inc. (1995)

Dunas, Felice. *Passion Play* Riverhead Trade (1998)

Engel, Beverly. *The Power of Apology: Healing Steps to Transform All Your Relationships.* New York: John Wiley & Sons (2001)

Foa, Edna, & Reid Wilson. *Stop Obsessing! How to Overcome Your Obsession and Compulsions.* New York: Bantam Books (1991)

Felder, Leonard. *Wake Up or Break Up: 8 Crucial Steps to Strengthening Your Relationship.* Rodale Books (2005)

Greer, Jane & Margery Rosen. *How Could You Do This to Me? Learning Trust After Betrayal.* New York: Broadway Books (2000)

Glass, Shirley P. & Jean Coppock Staeheli. *Not "Just Friends": Rebuilding Trust and Recovering Your Sanity After Infidelity.* New York: Free Press (2004)

Gottman, John M. *The Relationship Cure: A 5 Step Guide to Strengthening Your Marriage, Family and Friendships* New York, Three Rivers Press (2001)

Hendrix, Harville. *Getting the Love You Want: A Guide for Couples.* New York: Harper Perennial (1988)

Jampolsky, Gerald. *Love Is Letting Go of Fear, Third Edition.* Berkeley: Celestial Arts (2010)

Jampolsky, Gerald. *Forgiveness: The Greatest Healer of All.* Hillsboro: Atria Books/Beyond Words (1999)

Johnson, Sue. *Hold Me Tight: Seven Conversations for a Lifetime of Love.* New York: Little, Brown and Company (2008)

Katie, Byron. *Loving What Is: Four Questions that Can Change Your Life* New York: Three Rivers Press (2002)

Lambrou, Peter & George Pratt. *Code to Joy: The Four-Step Solution to Unlocking Your Natural State of Happiness.* New York: Harper One (2012)

Lenton, A. P. & Bryan, A. *An affair to remember: The role of sexual scripts in perceptions of sexual intent.* Personal Relationships. 12, 483-98. (2005).

Michael, R. T., Gagnon J. H., Laumann, E. O., & Kolata, G. *Sex in America.* Boston: Little, Brown. (1994)

Orloff, Judith. *Emotional Freedom: Liberate Yourself From Negative Emotions and Transform Your Life.* Three River Press (2010)

Newberg, Andrew, M.D. & Mark Robert Waldman. *How God Changes Your Brain: Breakthrough Findings by a Leading Neuroscientist* (Ballantine, 2010)

Notarius, Clifford & Howard Markman. *We Can Work It Out: How to Solve Conflicts, Save Your Marriage, and Strengthen Your Love for Each Other* New York: Perigee (1993)

Pittman, Frank. *Private Lies: Infidelity and the Betrayal of Intimacy.* New York: W.W. Norton & Company (1990)

Richo, David. *How to be An Adult in Relationships: The Five Keys to Mindful Loving.* Boston: Shambhala (2002)

Subotnik, Rona & Gloria Harris. *Surviving Infidelity: Making Decisions, Recovering from the Pain.* Avon: Adams Media Corp (1999)

Vaughan, Peggy. *The Monogamy Myth: A Personal Handbook for Recovering from Affairs.* New York: Newmarket Press (2003)

Additional Resources on the Net

Cherie Burbach. *Friendship vs. Emotional Affair: Signs Your Friendship Has Crossed Into Questionable Territory:* http://datingadvice.suite101.com/article.cfm/friendship_vs_emotional_affair

Heather Johnson Durocher. *Are You Having an Emotional Affair?* http://www.redbookmag.com/print-this/emotional-affair-ll

Jeanie Lerche Davis. *Cheating Wives: Women and Infidelity:* http://www.webmd.com/sex-relationships/guide/cheating-wives-women-infidelity

Sheri Meyers. *The 3A's: Keeping the Romance Alive:* http://www.straightfromtheheart.com/growth_keepingromancealive.htm

Peggy Vaughan. *Questions about Monogamy.* available at http://www.dearpeggy.com/monogamy.html

Sue Shallenbarger. *Co-Workers Can Wreck a Marriage: At the Office, Divorce is Contagious,* WALL ST. J., Nov. 12, 2003, at D1, available at http://www.careerjoumal.com/columnists/workfamily/ 20031114-work-family.html

The Truth About Infidelity: http://www.truthaboutdeception.com/quizzes/public/infidelity_statistics.html

Cheating Spouse - Facts, Information and Advice: http://www.truthaboutdeception.com/cheating_spouse/public/cheating_spouse.html

Cheating Wife - Facts and Advice: http://www.truthaboutdeception.com/cheating_spouse/public/cheating_wife.html

Many Cheat for a Thrill, More Stay True for Love: http://www.msnbc.msn.com/id/17951664/ns/health-sexual_health/t/many-cheat-thrill-more-stay-true-love/

Body Language of a Liar: http://www.humanliedetection.com/BodyLanguageOfLiars.php

Take the Love Language Quiz: http://www.5lovelanguages.com/assessments/love/

Here are 3 web sites designed by Dr. Sheri that are filled with helpful videos, related articles, blogs, and free gifts for you.

Please visit Dr. Sheri at
ChattingorCheating.com
www.StraightFromTheHeart.com
www.DrSheri.com

INDEX

ABOUT THE AUTHOR

Sheri Meyers, Psy.D., a licensed Marriage & Family Therapist, is among the national media's most frequently quoted and interviewed relationship, infidelity and life transition experts. For over 25 years, Dr. Sheri has used her expertise to help thousands of men and women face and overcome their most complex and life-wrenching relationship challenges with honesty, dignity, and love.

Consequently, Dr. Sheri has become a highly sought-after relationship and infidelity expert for broadcast network news (ABC, NBC, CBS, FOX), cable TV (Lifetime, CNN, E! Entertainment), internet portals (Videojug, YouTube, Blip) and on numerous television and radio entertainment programs and advice shows.

Dr. Sheri hosted and produced the weekly relationship television talk show *'Straight From The Heart'* for 11 years—a show dedicated to helping viewers enrich their lives, boost their love potential and enhance their relationships.

In the cyber world, as the Videojug.com online love, marriage and infidelity expert, Dr. Sheri has filmed hundreds of video segments answering peoples most personal and controversial questions about love, sex, communication, adultery, jealousy, power struggles and other problems areas that arise in relationships. Thousands of visitors watch and are helped by these online videos daily.

Both in her private practice and in front of national television audiences, Dr. Sheri is known for her knack of transforming the FEAR of change into the FUN of change. With intelligence, compassion and straight talk, she gets to the heart of the matter and shows people how to make healthy decisions in order to seize the life and love they have always wanted.

In *'Chatting or Cheating,'* Dr. Sheri shares with you her exclusive and unique insights that come from a wealth of experience in lovingly counseling, helping and inspiring thousands of couples to successfully heal, as they navigate though the murky and often dangerous waters of **EMOTIONAL SEX** and all forms of **INFIDELITY**.

For helpful tips, informative videos, free gifts, and more information

Please visit Dr. Sheri at

www.ChattingorCheating.com

CPSIA information can be obtained at www.ICGtesting.com
Printed in the USA
LVOW100030061212

310330LV00012B/249/P